T0246061

PRAISE FOR *LET'S GO!*

"Jamie Ramsden leads by example, and *Let's Go!* reflects his expertise in truly understanding what it takes to be a great leader. His extraordinary ability to 'emotionally' connect our senior leadership team was like nothing I've ever experienced before. Simply remarkable!"

—*Robert Chavez, Executive Chairman, Hermès Americas*

"A must-read! The Adastra Leadership Model is truly groundbreaking and has had a profound impact on my own leadership journey. I highly recommend *Let's Go!* to anyone looking to take their leadership to the next level."

—*Vanessa LeFebvre, President, Champion – Global*

"Jamie Ramsden packs a career of operational excellence and profound leadership coaching into a must-read for all current and aspiring leaders. For anyone on a leadership journey, *Let's Go!* is your guidebook—I'll be reading this book again and again."

—*Matt Baer, CEO, Stitch Fix*

"Jamie Ramsden's leadership philosophy and approach are truly exceptional and deserve to be studied and implemented by leaders everywhere. My personal experience with him has been nothing short of transformative, marking a pivotal turning point in my own leadership journey. I highly recommend *Let's Go!* to anyone seeking to enhance their leadership skills and make a meaningful impact on their teams and organizations."

—*Tameeka Smith, CEO, VA Community Plan, UnitedHealthcare*

"Only Jamie Ramsden, drawing on years of top-level executive coaching, could have so clearly articulated the core principles of leadership in a way that is both insightful and actionable. Something useful in every chapter."

—*Reade Fahs, CEO, National Vision, Inc.*

"Jamie Ramsden has masterfully developed a holistic yet simple view to leadership, and a practical modern approach to unlock your most powerful leadership traits. His leadership model is an absolute 'must' for any executive leading teams or organizations."

—*Ana Garcia, CEO, Kinetico*

"I have known Jamie Ramsden professionally as an extraordinary executive coach and CEO for over 15 years. He has delivered impactful, life-changing results to leaders and teams globally, often partnering with the Center for Creative Leadership. Now, he has authored a terrific leadership book based on his personal leadership model that will assist leaders at every level to grow vertically and accomplish great things as they help Shape the Future."

—*VADM John Ryan USN Ret. and former CEO, Center for Creative Leadership*

"Jamie weaves together practical and accessible strategies for leaders with an incisive point of view on what it really takes to shape a better future. The depth, pragmatism, and inspiring lessons in this book leave the reader feeling empowered and mobilized for action. Leaders, let's go!"

—*Jonathan Kirschner, Psy.D., Founder & CEO of AIIR Consulting*

"Jamie both challenged my thinking and supported me in ways that were responsive in real-time to the pandemic's historic challenges. Now, through *Let's Go!*, leaders the world over will benefit from the wisdom he has gained—and codified within the Adastra Leadership Model—as a CEO and an outstanding executive leadership coach."

—*Kevin Hinton, CEO & Executive Director, Beacon House*

"*Let's Go!* is a practical guide to leadership for managers, vice presidents, and chief executives alike because the content speaks to universal human needs. The book's useful model helped me understand how to best leverage my leadership roles, and I lead more successfully—and comfortably—as a result."

—*Khoa Dao, CEO, Australia Pacific LNG*

"Great leaders shape the future, rather than waiting for it to happen. The Adastra model brilliantly connects leaders with their mission, context, and people, to deliver real change, impact, and progress."

—*Peter Fisk, Professor at IE Business School and Author of* Business Recoded *and* The Complete CEO

"Jamie's leadership model captures aspects of human motivation that are essential to all leaders, wherever they operate. My career has benefited, and so will you."

—*Shalima Pannikode, Chair, AFRJ Freedom Council*

"A powerful leadership framework derived from Jamie's global experience. There's a real nugget of wisdom in each chapter."

—*Richard Bartlett, CEO, bp pulse*

"Moving from a startup to a scale up as both co-founder and CEO requires rethinking both internal and external thoughts and behaviors. Jamie's approach and direct feedback helped me understand that what got me here was not going to get me where I, and my team, needed me to be. The application of his leadership model to my challenges has made a real impact not only to my effectiveness, but my purpose and happiness as well."

—*Alexander García-Tobar, CEO & Co-founder, Valimail*

"Working with Jamie was eye-opening. Even though I was an experienced leader with over 25 years in my industry, he helped shape my thinking to a higher level, benefiting my team and the organization. Jamie's book captures the essence of leadership and how to perform at your best personally and professionally."

—*Marcie Williams, CEO, RKW Residential*

"Jamie's insights about where to focus my time and energy, and how to create space to lead with confidence and conviction, have been invaluable to me stepping into my new role as CEO. His leadership model is simple, yet powerful!"

—*John Gaither, CEO, Feetures*

"Jamie has been a trusted executive coach for several members of our senior team, including myself. His insights and practical advice are always spot-on, and he has made a huge, positive difference in my own leadership development, as well as that of my team. Jamie, as usual, hits all the right notes in *Let's Go!* Aspiring and seasoned leaders alike will benefit greatly from his tremendous ability to communicate in highly relatable and actionable concepts that touch the core of true leadership."

—*John M. Carrigg, President & CEO, United Health Services*

"Jamie's book makes a compelling case for the Adastra Leadership Model—which intertwines our underlying human needs with our roles as leaders and then outlines the key competencies required to ensure effectiveness. This book is a must-read for all leaders looking to fully understand their roles and maximize their leadership potential in a very pragmatic and straightforward manner."

—*Ross Dupper, President & CEO, Porsche Financial Services, Inc.*

"What an inspiration this book is—so affirming of every person's capacity and responsibility to lead, to positively influence. Jamie Ramsden's CEO experience and leadership model captured in this book was game changing for me in my first year as president and has given me the tools to understand my strengths, weaknesses and how to untap my vision for my future."

—*Sean O'Connor, President, Universal Furniture*

"If you're ready to elevate your leadership journey, Jamie Ramsden's *Let's Go!* is a must-read. This book goes beyond traditional leadership narratives, offering a roadmap for shaping the future. Having Jamie as my executive coach has been a transformative experience, and his guidance, now encapsulated in this book, is a beacon for anyone aspiring to lead with purpose and impact. Let's go, indeed!"

—Jen Shepherd, Global Head, Uber Transit

"Jamie Ramsden coaches how to leverage your time, team, and energy. He has helped me practice becoming the best leader and person I can be."

—Andrew Grauer, CEO & Cofounder, Learneo

"To this day, I call Jamie my 'Ranger Buddy,' which is a US Army Ranger School term that describes someone you can trust and count on in the most difficult situations. When I was transitioning from tactical, operational leadership to strategic leadership as the president of an organization—while also going through significant personal and professional adversity—Jamie's guidance was instrumental. His leadership model is outstanding for leaders at all levels, and I highly recommend learning from his experiences in *Let's Go!*"

—Clay Daniels, former Green Beret and President,
U.S. Engineering Service

"Jamie Ramsden's book *Let's Go!* is spot-on! He takes a refreshingly modern approach to demonstrating that great leaders are not born. Rather, through a core set of principles, they can be developed to confront today's challenges. From his conceptual leadership model to the supporting roles and competencies, this book is applicable to emerging leaders forging their paths... to seasoned executives looking to sharpen their skills!"

—J. Michael Parnell, Ph.D., President & CEO,
UnitedHealthcare of Mississippi, Inc.

"Jamie Ramsden's new book *Let's Go!* is an incredible distillation of the key roles that he espouses as critical for effective leadership. The book was a great refresher of the impactful learnings I took away from the time I spent with Jamie as my coach and mentor.

I enthusiastically recommend *Let's Go!* to current and aspiring leaders—there is always more to learn and more to practice."

—*Robert Mandel, President, Carelon Medical Benefits Management and Carelon Post Acute Solutions*

"Jamie's leadership model brings to life the many ways leaders have impact, and the importance of adapting communication styles to fit the context. This is only possible with intentional preparation, and his model helps leaders focus on doing the work upfront for better outcomes later."

—*Heather Brilliant, CEO and President, Diamond Hill Capital Management*

"As a female executive, working with Jamie has been a game changer because he pairs no-nonsense advice and tailored solutions with true compassion and understanding, no matter the complexity. His greatest hits are front and center in *Let's Go!*"

—*Kristin Ciriello Pothier, Life Sciences Sector Leader, KPMG and Author of* Personalizing Precision Medicine

"Having worked with Jamie Ramsden for years as a coach it is great to see him bringing his leadership wisdom to print. In this dynamic, post-COVID environment, the insights presented in *Let's Go!* are very much needed. This is a book not to be missed by anyone trying to navigate the leadership challenges of our time."

—*Kenneth Roberts, President, Atlas Roofing Company*

"*Let's Go!* represents the definitive guide for leaders seeking to disrupt, innovate, and create diverse, high-performing cultures. Jamie Ramsden masterfully utilizes trusted frameworks, and decades of coaching experience, to demonstrate how metrics for winning include both shareholder returns and stakeholder value."

—*Jason Wingard, Ph.D., Executive Chairman, The Education Board, Inc., Distinguished Visiting Professor, Harvard University and Author,* The Great Skills Gap: Optimizing Talent for the Future of Work

"Framed around an intellectually robust and research-driven model, Jamie engagingly helps leaders make sense of themselves, their experiences, their dreams, and their ambitions. The book works like a leadership prism refracting these into different glimpses of leadership done well. Behind the stories of organisational success lies the handmaiden of excellent leadership. Few books can translate how this occurs. Jamie has nailed it."

—Steve Kempster, Professor Emeritus, Lancaster University Management School

"Jamie's book is so complementary to the work he does for our company as an executive coach. Our leaders choose Jamie time and time again based on his experience, his coaching/leadership approach, and his profound relatability. He's got the rare gift of IQ and EQ."

—Heather Hrap, SVP, HR and REFS, ConocoPhillips

"Under Jamie Ramsden's coaching, my leadership evolved to an all-time high; *Let's Go!* mirrors the transformative strategies pivotal to my leadership success."

—Richard D. Consoli, Retired President, Cross Precision Measurement Group and Community Servant

"Jamie Ramsden's *Let's Go!* is a comprehensive guide, highlighting modern leadership challenges and providing the reader with useful solutions. Skillfully crafted, the book offers a refreshing and unique perspective, making it a standout among today's more traditional leadership literature. The innovative yet practical four-dimensional model introduced in the book not only aligns well with current management practices, but also proposes transformative strategies that promise to redefine what it means to be an effective leader. *Let's Go!* is an essential read for anyone looking to enhance their skill set and successfully navigate the evolving demands of contemporary leadership roles."

—Mike Rucker, Ph.D., Author of The Fun Habit

"Jamie is the epitome of professionalism, and I couldn't be any more positive about his impact on the leaders he coaches. He's the best 'coach role model' I have ever worked with."

—*Kent S. Price III, Former Chief Human Resources Officer, Center for Creative Leadership*

"I had the privilege of working with Jamie almost 30 years ago, where we had profound and stimulating discussions on leadership. His compelling book covers very logically and precisely the elements required of a leader to inspire people to make value-creating decisions, whether in for-profit or not-for-profit organisations. Essential reading for anyone wanting to soak in insightful, universal, practical observations and understandings of leadership."

—*Andrew Robshaw, Author of* Thankonomics

"Having both benefited directly from Jamie's wisdom and collaborated with him in helping others, I've experienced the impact of the Adastra model firsthand. It's a comprehensive tool that guides leaders to be intentional and balanced with how and why they activate their superpowers."

—*Dan Gallagher, Founder and CEO, Gallagher Leadership and Author of* The Self-Aware Leader

"Jamie's new book shows the way for the next generation of leaders, which humanity desperately needs. We've worked together and I can vouch personally for the efficacy of his holistic, third way of thinking."

—*Dr. John Daniels, Vice Chancellor for Research and Chief Research Officer, UNC Charlotte*

LET'S GO!

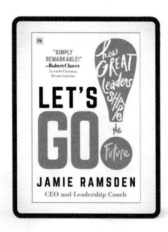

LET'S GO!

How Great Leaders Shape the Future

JAMIE RAMSDEN

Harriman House

HARRIMAN HOUSE LTD
3 Viceroy Court
Bedford Road
Petersfield
Hampshire
GU32 3LJ
GREAT BRITAIN
Tel: +44 (0)1730 233870

Email: enquiries@harriman-house.com
Website: harriman.house

First published in 2024.

Hardback ISBN: 978-1-80409-038-1
Paperback ISBN: 978-1-80409-075-6
eBook ISBN: 978-1-80409-039-8

British Library Cataloguing in Publication Data
A CIP catalogue record for this book can be obtained from the British Library.

To my parents, Mike and Sylv, who inspired me to live life to the fullest. Anyone who came through our doors at number 37 was met with the warmth of acceptance, the joy of music, a delight in community, the power of service, and unconditional love.

CONTENTS

CONTENTS

INTRODUCTION

WE'VE ALL SEEN it: In the face of real-world problems, high-flown leadership theories can disintegrate into airy abstraction. Not helpful. But we've also seen how purely reactive, in-the-moment problem-solving—with no reflection, no framework, no guiding vision—can create an unstable, patchwork organization held together with scotch tape. Also, not helpful—especially as a company grows and its problems get bigger and more complex.

That's exactly why this book blends theory and practical application. Both are essential.

Here's how I know. In the leadership space, executives do the work, coaches guide them to success, while academics study the field. Rarely do these roles overlap. But I've worn all three hats: executive, coach, and academic.

I spent a decade as an international CEO. I have an MBA specializing in leadership and change management. And for the last 20 years, I've been an elite coach, supporting hundreds of high-performing, high-impact, and high-potential leaders worldwide—mostly in the C-suite.

So, I can say with certainty that if you are, or aspire to be, an executive, a coach, or an academic, this book can help. Action-oriented executives will learn practical solutions to real-life business challenges. Coaches can leverage the book's content to fit their clients' needs. And executives, coaches, and academics can use my leadership model.

This book is designed to inspire. Much of my work involves helping leaders better understand themselves and their own motivations, as well as those of their team. Readers will acquire tools to help them in business, which they can also use to become better parents, partners, sons and daughters, friends, or community members. I want you to elevate your game and bring others along for the ride.

The first section takes a brief look at leadership theory to date, an overview that will help contextualize the second section, which outlines my own leadership model. Created at the turn of the century as part of my thesis on leadership, and refined during my work as a CEO and as an elite coach, the model explores four universal leadership dimensions.

Four sections based on those four leadership dimensions make up the book's core and lay out the four roles of a leader.

To begin with, each leader should demonstrate consistency and integrity to become a **Role Model** for their group or organization. The ability to focus on others, along with the connections that emerge with superior <u>communication</u> skills are two critical qualities for a leader who aims to become a **Community Builder** with like-minded, motivated supporters.

Great business, social, political, and community leaders also possess a <u>learning orientation</u> and high cognitive/social/emotional <u>intelligence</u> that allows them to become a **Sense Maker** during times of change. Finally, a leader is a **Future Shaper**. Future Shapers have a clear <u>vision</u> and an energetic, systemic <u>bias for action</u>. They create successful, sustainable, strategic—transformative—results for their teams by embracing and managing an uncertain future.

Each of the Role Model, Community Builder, Sense Maker, and Future Shaper sections contain ten short, stand-alone chapters with clear, compelling language geared toward busy executives—or anyone with a hectic life. You may prefer to read the book straight through for a more comprehensive take. Or cherry-pick content as it resonates with your role, stage of life, or personal challenges.

The book finishes with a guide to how the four leadership roles work together to help leaders achieve success in their professional and personal lives.

My hope is that you see yourself in these pages. I wrote this book to give you the tools to help you bring your dreams to fruition, while also providing inspiration for you, your team, and your organization to better understand yourselves and your purpose.

You can do what great leaders do. You can shape the future.

So let's go, leaders. Let's go!

AN INTENTIONALLY BRIEF HISTORY OF LEADERSHIP

TRADITIONAL LEADERSHIP RESEARCH has tended to focus on one or two dimensions. Most often, that's the single dimension of the leader's character and will, or the two-dimensional dynamic between either the leader and their followers *or* the leader and their organizational/ situational context.

There has been less focus on the three-dimensional interplay between the leader, their followers, and the context. That's where my own theory of leadership stands out. I focus on all three, and I add a critical fourth dimension as well: the future.

But let's begin with a look at previous approaches.

Great Man Theory

For most of human history, leadership roles have been dominated by physically strong, powerful individuals (yes, mostly men) who used command and control as the primary mechanism to drive successful outcomes. Proposed by Thomas Carlyle in the 19th century, the underlying principle of Great Man Theory is this: Leaders are born, not made.

Great Man Theory prevailed from early human tribes through the industrial revolution and continued into modern-era military organizations, government institutions, and corporate structures. Hereditary factors such as bloodline or physical presence and dominance—big, strong, loud—determined who led. Despite hundreds of years of social progress, these ideas still run deep.

Context-driven leadership

Even in the Great Man era, theorists recognized circumstances in which the context evoked leadership. Such leaders were "made" by the demands of the world around them and opportunistically rose to the occasion, regardless of bloodline or physical presence and dominance.

The French and American Revolutions are prime examples of how disruptive events initiated a contextual need for leaders to emerge. To paraphrase Abigail Adams, wife of second US president John Adams, great necessities call forth great leaders.

Situational leadership

In the mid- to late 20th century, the concept of leadership development—the belief that you can learn to be a leader, or a better one—emerged. Instead of looking at an individual's bloodline or physical presence and dominance, other critical factors are considered, namely: personality traits, natural preferences, and behaviors.

Here's where situational leadership enters the picture. The premise is that leaders can at least to some extent be "made" and can adapt their leadership style to a need or circumstance.

Follower-centered leadership

As a counterpoint to traditional hierarchical leadership models where the leader is at the top, in the late 20th century Robert Greenleaf identified the concept of "servant leadership." His approach is based on the idea that the most effective leaders should first and foremost serve others by making sure their needs are met. Others, or "followers" in leadership terms, are the primary focus.

Decentralized leadership principles like servant leadership prioritize the collective—by giving attention to and supporting an organization's frontline workers, for example—rather than the individual at the top. This style is prevalent in certain organizations, cultures, and parts of the world.

Postmodern leadership

Theoretically, postmodern leadership can describe a leadership paradigm where neither the leader nor the context is essential. A few thoughts…

- Co-leadership, where leadership roles are shared or rotated, offers flexibility and alternative perspectives. The style has been tried in a few corporations with mixed results. It might be more suitable for small groups.

- Our social-media-savvy, technology-driven world has introduced the opportunity for non-human leadership entities using AI, avatars, or leadership proxies.

- There are certain situations in which leadership does not manifest in an individual or recognizable form. Instead, it is dispersed, elusive, and emergent—more like a perceived reality of a faceless system: think George Orwell's "Big Brother."

MY LEADERSHIP MODEL

It's an exciting time in the evolution of leadership and leadership theory. But even as the world grows increasingly complex and uncertain, our basic needs as human beings remain unchanged.

People have always sought, and continue to seek, a sense of self, belonging, meaning, and purpose. And one of the distinctive aspects of my leadership model is that it speaks to these four universal human needs.

My leadership paradigm is uniquely grounded in a four-dimensional approach that emerges from these four universal human needs. I've included the individual or leader (sense of self), the team or followers (sense of belonging), and the context (sense of meaning). But I've also elevated and integrated the importance of a sense of purpose, the mission—the mission of shaping the future.

It may seem like a simple addition, but it's a transformative one. Let me show you why.

THE ADASTRA
LEADERSHIP MODEL

C REATED AT THE turn of the century as part of my thesis on leadership—and used and refined since then in my work as a CEO and as an elite coach—the Adastra Leadership Model links four universal leadership dimensions with four underlying human needs. The short version is this: Fulfilling your sense of *self*, sense of *belonging*, sense of *meaning*, and sense of *purpose* contributes to a successful life. And we look to our leaders to help us do just that.

The model is a cornerstone of my executive coaching and leadership development practice, Adastra Consulting. The company's name derives from the British Royal Air Force's motto: "Per ardua ad astra." It's an inspirational phrase that translates to "through adversity to the stars," and alludes to the underlying premise of the leader's journey—that you can't experience greatness without overcoming great challenge. Before we explore the Adastra Leadership Model, it's important to define its four dimensions of leadership: the individual (or leader), the team (or followers), the context, and the mission as seen in Figure 1.

FIGURE 1: THE ADASTRA LEADERSHIP MODEL'S FOUR DIMENSIONS

You'll see that the individual—or the leader—is the connecting hub. There is a back-and-forth interplay between the individual and the team, the individual and the context, and the individual and the mission.

Out of these four dimensions—these four areas of interplay—emerge the four roles of a leader, as shown in Figure 2. Each role connects to one of the four underlying human needs, and each defines how the leader should show up in those four areas: in other words, what *competencies* are required to fulfill the leadership roles.

FIGURE 2: THE ADASTRA LEADERSHIP MODEL'S FOUR ROLES AND ASSOCIATED COMPETENCIES

Let's explore these four roles in greater detail.

People seek out authentic leaders who bring out the best version of themselves. Great leaders have presence, self-awareness, credibility, and consistency, which motivates people to develop their own *sense of self.*

A group's leader reflects the values and ambitions of the people they represent. Those values and ambitions will be shaped by the context, but two will remain constant: Every leader should demonstrate <u>consistency</u> and <u>integrity</u>. That's the most effective way they can become a *role model* for their group or organization.

People look to leaders to help them feel connected to the collective, to become a part of something bigger than themselves. Great leaders communicate well, build great teams, develop others, and grow relationships to help people feel *a sense of belonging*.

Every leader should aim to become a *community builder* with like-minded, motivated supporters—not just inside their teams, but across their organizations, in conjunction with their partners, within their local communities, and across their wider industries.

That means honing the ability to <u>focus on others</u> as well as developing superior <u>communication</u> skills that create connections.

Intelligence
Learning Orientation
SENSE MAKER

People want leaders to help them understand and interpret the world. People need leaders to simplify complexity and ease decision-making, and a leader must bring perspective and sound judgment to that task. They learn through others and make sense of information to provide people with a greater *sense of meaning*.

This critical sense-making role makes high cognitive/social/ emotional <u>intelligence</u> essential for a leader. Great business, social, political, and community leaders also possess a <u>learning orientation</u> that allows them to become *sense makers* during times of change.

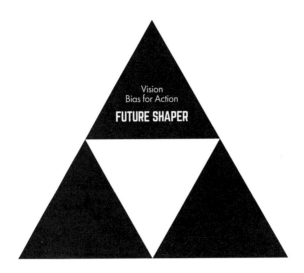

People turn to leaders to build a better tomorrow, to help them leave a mark by having a dream and bringing it to life. Great leaders are purposeful and strategic, and they use a compelling vision to lead change, which gives people a deeper *sense of purpose.*

That's why a leader orients toward the future. A leader is a *future shaper.* Future shapers have a clear <u>vision</u> and an energetic, systemic <u>bias for action</u>. The results they create for their teams are successful, sustainable, and strategic—in a word, transformative. And they do it by embracing and managing an uncertain future.

A HIGH-LEVEL SUMMARY

Table 1 concisely summarizes the Adastra Leadership Model's dimensions, roles, competencies, and underlying needs.

TABLE 1: DIMENSIONS, ROLES, COMPETENCIES, AND UNDERLYING NEEDS

Dimension	Role	Competencies	Need
The Leader	Role Model	Consistency Integrity	Sense of Self
The Team	Community Builder	Communication Focus on Others	Sense of Belonging
The Context	Sense Maker	Intelligence Learning Orientation	Sense of Meaning
The Mission	Future Shaper	Vision Bias for Action	Sense of Purpose

This may seem a bit abstract, but hang in there, because it's what underpins everything you're about to read. As you go through the rest of the book, keep in mind how these fundamental human needs endure in almost every leadership situation.

Let's get into it.

THE LEADER AS A ROLE MODEL

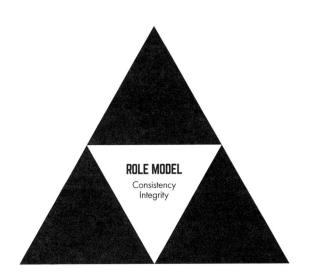

ROLE MODEL
Consistency
Integrity

THIS SECTION CONSIDERS the individual dimension of leadership.

As we touched on in the last section, a group's leader reflects the values and ambitions of the people they represent. Those values and ambitions will be shaped by the context, but two will remain constant: Every leader should demonstrate consistency and integrity. That's the most effective way they can become a *role model* for their group or organization.

KEY COMPETENCIES

Integrity

Having a strong set of principles and values that reflect the people the leader has been chosen to represent.

Consistency

When leaders do what they say and say what they do, it builds trust.

IN SHORT

People seek out authentic leaders who bring out the best version of themselves. Great leaders have presence, self-awareness, credibility, and consistency, which motivates people to develop their own *sense of self.*

As you read through the next ten chapters, think about how you show up as a Role Model. How developed is your sense of self? In what ways will you develop others' sense of self? How will you bring out the best in people?

CREATE SPACE FOR LEADERSHIP

TASKED WITH SOLVING real-time, tactical challenges and putting out fire after fire after fire, managers focus on action. In a fast-paced, time-starved culture that rewards people for getting things done, the idea of leaving deliberate schedule gaps for uninterrupted thought may feel uncomfortable, unfamiliar—or just unattainable. Many managers judge themselves, and consider themselves to be judged, by the fullness of their calendar.

But there can be no strategic intent without deliberate contemplation. For managers to become leaders, deeper reflection is critical. And it is impossible to think clearly and deeply while in the middle of the arena, in the midst of battle.

Reflecting requires creating space: space in your calendar and in your head. And establishing that space—the space in which you'll build the future world that you, your team, and your company will live in—requires deliberate thought and action. Here's a start:

- Release control by trusting others on your team. This may be hard to do—extremely hard. But becoming a leader depends on it.

- Reprioritize ongoing activities like team meetings and group updates. Important and urgent ones come first, non-essential and incidental ones come last (or not at all).

- Leverage available tools. To begin with, look at time-saving technology and delegating to teams.

- Say no to work that you can delegate, defer, reprioritize, outsource, or let go.

- Make a habit of blocking out thinking time.

Great leaders think more than they act. Before they focus on growth, they push the world back by slowing things down. Intentionally creating space helps leaders identify future needs and determine how the organization will meet them. It also allows them to:

Move beyond task-oriented thinking

Reflection: How do the tasks, projects, or initiatives fit into the bigger picture?

Build relationships

Reflection: How can I build a deep, powerful network *before* I actually need it?

Cultivate threat awareness

Reflection: What competitive conditions positively or negatively affect the organization?

Understand the wider business environment

Reflection: What client or macro-environmental conditions positively or negatively affect the organization?

Build out organizational capabilities

Reflection: What resources or competencies should the business develop *before* it needs to perform even more successfully?

Expand services

Reflection: What products and services does the market need? Which ones may they not even know about yet?

Identify future investment opportunities

Reflection: What is the best use of the organization's current and future resources?

Grow people

Reflection: How am I challenging and supporting our people to build teams for the future?

Leadership requires a different mindset than managing. If you could spend time each day reflecting, how much better could you perform? How much more prepared would you be to navigate an uncertain future?

Organizations need leaders because situations require leadership. And if you're not leading, who is?

INTENTIONS ARE WORTH MORE THAN GOALS

MANY OF US have been fed the same recipe for success: Set a goal then work hard to meet it. Although this two-step approach is obvious, even simplistic, it often fails, especially in the long term—and the long term must be top of mind for leaders.

Take the most typical of New Year's resolutions: the goal of losing weight.

People usually begin by suppressing comfortable and learned behaviors. Out goes the TV binging, donuts, and beer; in come 6am runs, kale salads, and superfood smoothies. That's the hard work.

Some people will stay on track toward their weight loss goals, but by the time February rolls around, many will be falling short. Failure sets the stage for negative self-talk. "I'm a quitter." "I lack determination." "I'm not good enough." The usual self-defeating classics.

The apparent winners are not immune to failure, either, at least not in the long term. After the initial goal is achieved, those suppressed, comfortable behaviors start to creep back in. Pretty soon, as rapidly as it was lost, all the weight returns. The internal critic plays its soundtrack full blast.

Why do so many people fail? Because focusing on a singular goal is short-term, transactional thinking; which leads to unsustainable results.

Think about it this way: You can bail water out of a boat, but if you never get to the root problem—*how is the water coming in?*—the boat will inevitably fill up again. When you have a narrow, singular goal, you ignore crucial variables in the ecosystem; you zero in on outputs instead of inputs.

Transformational, sustainable change requires long-term, systemic thinking—a shift in perspective toward intentions and away from short-term goals. There's a huge difference.

Take that New Year's resolution to lose weight.

Instead of setting a fixed goal to lose a "magic number" of pounds, craft a broad, high-level intention to have a healthier lifestyle. Then create a system of realistic actions—like spending more time outside, playing tennis, or running a

5k with your spouse—that will serve your intention. Losing weight will be a welcome by-product.

Long-term thinking also means aligning your "why" with your intention. Why do you want to have a healthier lifestyle? Is it to enjoy time together with your spouse? To be part of a wider community? To mitigate a genetically predisposed condition? Simply to enjoy more of life?

This matters, because "why" is where many people get stuck. They've been conditioned to answer "what," "where," "when," and "how" questions. In other words, to take short-term actions to reach specific goals. The deeper, inner work of aligning your "why" with your intention is worth the effort. It can take you where you want to go, maybe to places you've never imagined.

We've been fed that outdated recipe for success in the workplace, too.

Employees are trained, incentivized, recognized, and rewarded for hitting short-term targets. That traps them in a pattern similar to the dieting example: Transactional thinking that leads to tactical goal-setting; short-term behaviors ("let's just grind out this deadline") that lead only to unsustainable, temporary wins (if any); followed by long-term failure (deteriorating attitudes, diminished energy, lower production, quitting).

To achieve transformational, sustainable change, leaders must:

- Dig deep and figure out the "why." *Why is this change necessary?*

- Clearly define and communicate the "why" to themselves and their teams.

- Connect the "why" to the more tactical "what," "where," "when," and "how" questions. And then help the team see the connections between its purpose and actions.

A great leader does not simply perform actions in service of a goal. Instead, their every action springs from a deeper, more meaningful intention—a "why." This purposeful way of being can transform individual and team behaviors, and that growth has the potential to become sustainable, far-reaching, and impactful.

WHAT WE FEAR MOST

SOCIAL PSYCHOLOGIST DANIEL Wegner's ironic process theory, known as "The White Bear Problem," works like this: If I tell you *not* to think about a white bear, you will be unable to get the image of a white bear out of your mind. The harder you try to suppress thinking about a white bear, the more likely that specific thought is to emerge. You are probably thinking about a white bear now!

In a related—albeit more subtle—universal pattern, we unconsciously create the conditions for what we most fear. What begins as a defense mechanism meant to protect us from potential problems instead, in the long term, draws us toward the very future we are consciously trying to avoid.

In the workplace, this tendency commonly shows up in the following forms:

Control

Some leaders make a career out of creating certainty, a behavior often driven by a fear of being out of control. What might have made sense in a smaller organization or different department becomes a deep anxiety driving an over-involvement in the specifics. Even as their job scope and responsibilities increase, these stressed individuals continue to oversee every last variable to such a detailed extent that they're left with too much to manage. *The leader has created the perfect conditions for what they fear most: losing control.*

Avoiding conflict

Other leaders, bent on avoiding damaging internal conflicts that have killed more than one company, play down necessary dynamic tension among employees. Consequently, the team doesn't communicate in a challenging yet authentic manner. In the absence of these minor "course corrections," conflict drives down deep. The culture becomes passive, even passive aggressive. Interactions become transactional and genuine conversations are shelved until, eventually, team conflicts flare up dangerously. *The leader has created the perfect conditions for what they fear most: conflict.*

Inaction

Risk-averse leaders may be afraid of uncertainty. In many business situations, caution is a virtue. But over time, cautiousness may lead to decreased creativity. After years of sticking to established approaches and offering the same old products and services, customer relationships stagnate, competitors get ahead, and markets evolve, which exposes the organization to the biggest risk of all: the risk of doing nothing. *The leader has created the perfect conditions for what they fear most: uncertainty.*

Lack of trust

Healthy skepticism with an eye on reality is a virtue in a leader, but it can go too far. Leaders who don't trust their team, bosses, or clients can be driven by a fear of being taken advantage of. Their unwillingness to behave transparently, or to give others the benefit of the doubt, creates a mirrored lack of trust from others. A lack of trust means there's no intimacy, vulnerability, or confidence within the team. Just withholding. *The leader has created the perfect conditions for what they fear most: not being trusted.*

Constant judgment

Convinced that they are victims of unfair judgment, some leaders react by criticizing their colleagues. That's not the kind of clear-sighted analysis necessary in business. And colleagues and employees won't fail to pick up on it. Deflecting blame is contagious and creates an environment of escalating criticism; the culture erodes accordingly. *The leader has created the perfect conditions for what they fear most: being judged and worse, infecting those around them with blame and judgment.*

Prioritizing results over connections

Good leaders work hard and hope to see results. But a leader who's obsessed with driving for results is typically motivated by a fear of failure. By being intense and directive, they drive those around them to deliver short-term results. Their working relationships become transactional, with delivering results more important than making and sustaining connections. After a while, that lack of connection actually reduces the team's ability to produce sustainable results. *The leader has created the perfect conditions for what they fear most: a drop-off in results and, ultimately, failure.*

Resistance to change

By sticking only with the familiar, a leader who fears changing misses out on growth opportunities. When they resist being changed from the inside-out, through self-improvement, these individuals grow vulnerable to change from the outside-in: from clients, technologies, competitors, and industry innovation. *The leader has created the perfect conditions for what they fear most: being changed.*

Avoid the tendency to create the conditions for what you most fear by becoming self-aware. Look at the underlying causes of your own fear and focus on what you want, otherwise you'll be at the mercy of what you don't want. It takes a lot of work to identify patterns and to break age-old habits, but with focused intention, dedication, and a good guide, it's possible.

Buddhist teacher, author, and nun Pema Chödrön says, "Nothing ever goes away until it has taught us what we need to know." Only when we no longer serve our fears can we render them irrelevant.

BEWARE OF THE PSYCHOLOGICAL FOUR HORSEMEN

"**I** FEEL GUILTY ABOUT..."

"I regret deciding that..."

"I'm afraid of what might happen if..."

"I'm anxious about whether I can..."

Guilt. Regret. Fear. Anxiety. The psychological four horsemen of the apocalypse.

It's a somewhat playful description. But when we allow these emotions to shape our thinking—if we let them run the show—it's no laughing matter. The four horsemen do nothing but rob us of joy, but when we take charge of them, they can be turned to our benefit.

Guilt and regret

Thinking in binary terms of good or bad is rarely productive. When you view your actions through guilt and regret, highly emotive words that suggest you did something wrong, you're viewing actions through a negative lens, so you always see them as bad. A bad investment, a bad relationship, a bad choice.

Guilt and regret are connected to the past. We often convince ourselves that if we had made different decisions, our life would be better. But since we can't actually see the life we never lived, we can never completely know.

Fear and anxiety

Fear and anxiety are connected to the future. Giving these emotions weight can distort our thinking.

You may assume that the least desirable outcome is the one with the greatest probability, but ask yourself how often your fears have correctly predicted the future, and the answer is probably "almost never."

We stress about decisions that will affect the future. We play out a million different scenarios in our minds. What should we do? What should we say? How should we feel? But the truth is, we have no control over the future. The world is in constant flux.

"IN THE GRIP"

Whenever we experience guilt, regret, fear, and anxiety, we are in a state of high emotional alert. These responses to previous failures and perceived threats evolved long ago, when life was far more dangerous and threatening—think tigers and starvation rather than "I embarrassed myself" or "I lost a deal."

The occasional times in today's world when those primal reactions prevent real problems—the modern equivalent of being eaten by a tiger or starving—that's great. But it's much more common that guilt, regret, fear, and anxiety will cause us to be "in the grip": trapped by the past or paralyzed by the future.

If you're "in the grip," you can't think clearly and your ability to learn is diminished. You engage in unproductive self-talk. Sometimes, you can't act—at all. Often, you fail. And when you're surrounded by people who amplify your darkest thoughts, everything feels so much worse.

Unless we are ready to learn from being "in the grip," the psychological four horsemen serve no purpose.

If you want to benefit from feeling guilt and regret, you'll first need to acknowledge that rarely is anything ever 100% bad or 100% good. Then figure out what you can learn and how you can become better from that experience.

Most importantly, don't repeat past mistakes—do something different next time!

Learning from your feelings of fear and anxiety is a more nuanced process. The first step is fast-forwarding. What's the absolute worst-case scenario? And if that happens... how bad is it, really, and can I live with the consequences? Next, determine what the indicators are that you are on the wrong path. What is the probability of the worst-case scenario happening? If you see things going downhill, can you stop the descent?

There are usually far more steps from here to there than we imagine.

Asking these questions works best if you do it in a calm, thoughtful way rather than in a panicked, obsessive way. Remember: You always have the choice to step away from the situation and think rationally. If this doesn't come naturally, find a trusted partner to help.

Once you've gathered this information, stop worrying and press play. Go for it!

We can begin to tame guilt, regret, fear, and anxiety when we are aware of how they shape our thinking. If we're learning from those emotions and our thinking calms, we can show ourselves grace in letting go of the past. We'll also be able to create a structured plan to reduce future uncertainty.

As for those psychological four horsemen, they can ride off into the sunset, leaving us to truly enjoy the moment.

BECOME A
BENEVOLENT
DISRUPTOR

L EADERS IN A new role—recently promoted, recently
hired—usually act in one of two ways. Either their urgent
need to make an impact gives them a manic drive for results
or they feel intimidated by the position's responsibility
and scope.

In other words, they'll deal with change by exerting too
much or too little force on the organization's people,
processes, and culture. There's also a third, more balanced
way. Here's a look at all three.

THE CHANGE AGENT

Most leaders fit into the Change Agent category, because the most common leadership profile includes traits like *driven, action-oriented, ambitious,* and *impact-focused.* No wonder that Change Agents use a *push* approach to change!

A directive style can be useful in a crisis or other time-starved situations when there's little opportunity or need to build deep relationships. But outside of these special circumstances, telling others what to do—driving results in an overly prescriptive style—leads to resentment, active or passive resistance, and an erosion of trust.

Change Agents may also use aggressive communication to try to drive change. They might say things like:

- "Why the heck would we do it like this?"

- "What a stupid way of getting things done!"

- "This isn't how we did it at [my former company]."

Hostile language may get people to act immediately, but for those short-term wins, the leader is trading away long-term relationships. For instance, the Change Agent may attack a process without considering that the team may have (happily) used it for years, may even have created it.

In other words, the Change Agent hasn't taken the time to understand the background or paid attention to the specifics. Colleagues are likely to respond by disconnecting. They're not resisting change, they're resisting *being* changed—by having change thrust into their day-to-day work without their input or advice.

This leader has missed opportunities to build a "coalition of the willing." As a result, and even though the new direction may be better, progress slows. Initiatives are met with animosity, opposition, and in some cases, non-compliance.

So, the Change Agent doubles down and pushes harder. That leads to internal friction and frustration, ruptures in working relationships, and chaos.

Ultimately, the Change Agent may be removed as the new leader.

THE OUTSIDER

Outsiders use a *pull* approach to change. And in the early stages of integration, the pull approach can be helpful: gather information, ask questions, listen to opinions, draw out perspectives, and generally better understand the environment.

But while this may help build a foundation for longer-term success, only using an inquisitive "pull" style is less effective as an ongoing strategy.

Rather than acting, Outsiders observe. Stepping back can look like procrastination or indecisiveness. The new leader appears unwilling—or worse, unable—to manage conflict or drive decision-making.

For example, if there's a team conflict, the Outsider will gather information instead of acting. While the new leader may simply assume the situation will get better on its own, their non-action may be self-serving, intended to protect their own risk and reputation. Colleagues will pick up on that. They'll form opinions: ineffective, passive, uncaring, selfish.

This perceived lack of direction leads to internal friction and frustration, ruptures in working relationships, and chaos.

In some cases, this leader, too, is removed.

THE BENEVOLENT DISRUPTOR

An extreme push approach focuses on action. It increases the possibility of fractures from the inside-out—fractures within systems, people, and processes.

An extreme pull approach, passive and observing, means organizations don't benefit from planned, managed change from the inside-out. At the same time, it increases the likelihood of disruptive, uncertain change from the outside-in—from competition, clients, and other macro-economic factors.

Change is best effected through a third, more balanced approach, which blends the Change Agent and Outsider styles into something more flexible and impactful.

Benevolent Disruptors exercise judgment in when and how—and how much—they push and pull. These skilled leaders don't fancy themselves as Change Agents. Instead, they see themselves as change catalysts: facilitators who build internal coalitions which they then guide toward powerful, long-term external success.

Benevolent Disruptors don't stay at arm's length like Outsiders. They surface difficult conversations and develop relationships with intention and authenticity. They build early-stage alliances to generate team alignment and commitment. With team spirits high, wins come earlier and easier.

A Benevolent Disruptor changes the business for the better over the long term. They bring about change in an iterative and inclusive way, without breaking the methods and relationships that great organizations are founded on. They balance relationships and results in a way that brings out the best in the organization's people, processes, systems, and culture.

LOSING: ANOTHER WAY TO WIN

"IT'S EXCITING."

This is how the late basketball legend Kobe Bryant described what it feels like… to lose. "It means you have different ways to get better," he said. "There are certain things you can figure out—that you can take advantage of—certain weaknesses that were exposed that you need to shore up. So, it's exciting."

Hearing one of sport's greatest competitors describe losing as anything but unacceptable is surprising, but perhaps Kobe grew to understand that success is not linear, and that losing provides rich opportunities for growth. "It sucks to lose," he said, "but at the same time, there are answers there if you just look at them."

There are answers there if you just look at them.

Now of course, our professional lives don't typically present straightforward win-lose outcomes. We don't play one game at a time, and we use different scorecards and measures of success. Plus, most "wins" come with nuance. For example:

- A promotion is typically considered a victory. But what about the extra responsibility and increased pressure it puts on your work-life balance?

- When you win a big contract, you can feel triumphant in the moment. But right behind it, is that long task list...

But you do have this in common with the sporting greats: When you focus solely on the outcomes of your efforts, then it's black or white, win or lose. Either you accomplish your goals, or you don't. That means you miss out on what the more experienced Kobe seemed to know: Reflecting on your losses is one of the most important—and most exciting— parts of the game. As he said...

There are answers there if you just look at them.

LEARNING THROUGH ACTION

Learning through action is a long-term problem-solving approach that turns information into knowledge, and knowledge into wisdom. It is a cycle of doing and reflecting that helps you find better solutions before acting. Here's how it works.

STAGE 1: The event or the experiment

- These are concrete: everyday experiences—new or familiar—that you're personally involved in.

- Examples are launching a project, hosting a team retreat, or having a difficult conversation with a client.

STAGE 2: Observe and reflect

- Gather feedback from everyone involved. For instance, colleagues, clients, and others in the industry.

- Ask what did and did not go well—and more importantly, why.

STAGE 3: Identify options around improvement

- This is when you do a lot of thinking.

- For example: What alternative approaches can we

take to solve the problem? How can we overcome constraints? What will we do differently? How will the team work together better? What should we start/stop/continue doing?

- After you've exhausted all solutions, pick the best one.

- Make a commitment to act.

STAGE 4: Test it out

- There's no more discussion or reflection, just action.

- After you act, the learning loop restarts.

BENEFITS OF LEARNING THROUGH ACTION

Even when you don't get the instantaneous rewards of an immediate win, this approach can yield comprehensive—often transformative—benefits. You'll enjoy wider success beyond a singular event. You'll also be better equipped to:

- Think critically.

- Work collaboratively.

- Listen reflectively.

- Generate insights about the event or experience before acting.

- Formulate informed pathways to success.

ANOTHER WAY TO WIN

Learning through action leads to evolution and growth. You're gathering new information and building new skills. But you're also making connections. You're discovering relationships between your efforts, the team's efforts, external variables, and your context to understand how those relationships influence outcomes.

One of the things that made Kobe a legend was his ability to blend a performance mindset with what looked like a learning through action approach. He appeared to do this on the basketball court night after night, week after week, year after year, during the course of his career.

You can find a balance, too. By engaging in the process of appreciative inquiry, reflection, experimentation, and adaptation, you can transcend the limitations of the events and experiences that make up your life.

There are answers there if you just look at them.

BREAK THROUGH THE INVISIBLE FENCE

ONE AFTERNOON OVER two decades ago, during an afternoon walk in a suburban neighborhood, I spotted a lost dog in the middle of the road. When I approached, he didn't run off. Instead, the dog continued to stroll contentedly down the road until I caught up to him. He even let me check his tags.

I decided to walk "Boomer" home. After taking a firm hold of his collar, I led him back to his house, just a street away. And as we stepped into the front yard... ZAP! I shouted; Boomer squealed. Buzzing with electricity from crossing an invisible, electrified fence, together we limped across the grass. When we reached the front door, we were both still a little shaken up, still whimpering in pain.

OUR OWN INVISIBLE FENCES

I think about Boomer and the way he bravely broke through his invisible fence a lot, particularly when I'm helping clients overcome self-limiting thoughts and behaviors. Most of the time, this negative "stuff" is based on their formative personal and professional experiences.

Formative experiences are events that have a lasting influence on who we are. They are the shock, the blow, the jolt, the whammy. They shape the way we think and act in good ways. And not so good ways.

Maybe your parent constantly belittled you as a child. So you make yourself smaller and smaller until you're only doing things you know you can do right. You never stretch. But if your parent supported you, even when you made mistakes, even if you failed, you are less afraid to take risks.

Likewise, if your first boss unconditionally believed in you, that might make you more confident in your capabilities. Support without limitations means that we tend to see ourselves more positively. But if they didn't, you might doubt yourself.

Over time, your level of self-belief will manifest in one of two forms: strengthened friendships and an accelerated professional trajectory, or corroded relationships and a hindered career.

Your formative experiences—the ones that made you build invisible fences around yourself—are unique. But to evolve, you need to identify these limitations and work to turn that electricity off. In the meantime, you can break through them just like Boomer.

BREAKING ON THROUGH TO THE OTHER SIDE

Boomer wasn't unhappy when I first saw him. I know that now. He probably wasn't even lost! In retrospect, I see a dog exploring a wider world with an easy spirit and a contented heart—a dog for whom the initial shock was worth the payoff.

Feeling that initial shock takes courage. It's not easy to:

- Reach out for new relationships when you have been hurt.

- Push outside the boundaries of what has helped you cope in the past.

- Let go of actions and behaviors if you believe they are what has made you successful.

- Trust others if you have been let down.

- Try something new, if taking risks has led to embarrassment, humiliation, or shame.

Breaking through the invisible fences you've built around yourself will lead to short-term discomfort. That's a given. Yet if you choose to move beyond them as Boomer (that carefree and contented dog!) did, a whole new world can be within your reach.

It's been said that everything you want is on the other side of fear. So, go on. Brace yourself. Take a step. Or a leap! And break through the invisible fence.

EMBRACE YOUR NEMESIS

THERE'S SOMETHING ABOUT us in the people we don't like.

Why are you so irritated by that petty, judgmental neighbor? Why can your spouse laugh about them, while you brood, pettily, and judge them harshly? Why does that colleague who often interrupts make you want to set fire to the conference table—and how outrageous is it when others complain that you do the same thing?

The 13th-century Persian poet and scholar Rumi's take on this phenomenon has stood the test of time: "Many of the faults you see in others, dear reader, are your own nature reflected in them."

From myths to modern classics, heroes often battle outer foes that seem different, but who are actually closely linked to their inner demons. Think of Harry Potter and Voldemort— two ridiculed orphans, Parselmouths who speak snake and challenge the rules. Ultimately, Harry is tied to Voldemort as one of his "horcruxes," their intertwined souls hidden in plain sight.

Or Luke Skywalker and Darth Vader. Luke, who's drawn to the dark side, enters the Dark Side cave on Dagobah and has a vision of himself beheading Vader. Then, Vader's mask explodes, revealing Luke's own face. Later, in the antagonist-protagonist twist of the 20th century, Vader turns out to be Luke's flesh and blood—his father. But deep down, Luke has always known.

When there's a Voldemort or a Darth Vader in your real life—a challenging relative, a difficult friend, a tough client— they may trigger your own negative emotions. Your feelings about relationships, success, and commitment, for example. This concept, based on Carl Jung's Shadow Theory, argues that we suppress aspects of our personality we perceive as negative.

Integrating "The Shadow" leads to insight, self-confidence, and a deeper understanding of the human condition— essentially, growth. It is hard to pull off, but once we realize how others' behavior reflects both our own faults and the things within ourselves that we want to change, we can work toward not being triggered by it.

By spending time and being curious around the people who drive us crazy, we can learn about our own limitations and obtain a fuller appreciation of ourselves.

To stay calm when you're agitated:

- Understand where other people's behavior is coming from. All behavior, verbal and non-verbal, is communication.

- Accept that others' behavior may reflect our own faults and the things within ourselves that we want to change.

- Fight "white noise." Recognize when your inner voice is tangling you up in pessimistic, unproductive thinking. Then consciously work to reduce these distractions.

- Instead of reacting, respond with intention: Slow down, gather information, understand the context.

- When you finally act, adopt a "be like water" philosophy. Flow around the obstacles in your path.

- Leave judgments behind. If you can't do this completely, take time to make decisions.

The author Kahlil Gibran wrote: "And God said, 'Love Your Enemy,' and I obeyed him and loved myself."

To embrace a nemesis, to show compassion rather than judgment toward the things you dislike about yourself, is to choose to be the person the leader—you want to see in the world. What a powerful act of loving-kindness to bestow on others. What a gift to yourself.

DON'T BE A VICTIM
OF YOUR OWN BIAS

G ENDER, RACE, ETHNICITY, sexual orientation. Language, accent, education, upbringing. Organizational role, tenure, skillset, title. There are so many ways to feel different.

One client of mine, who described himself as an outsider, had plenty of reasons to feel different. He talked about cliquish co-workers whose narrow-minded judgments made doing good work impossible and blocked him from being part of the team.

My client responded by standing back from the group—nurturing his own grudges and criticisms—and ultimately, I strongly suspected, making himself difficult to work with.

For almost six months, this conversation happened repeatedly until one day, without prompt, they experienced a powerful insight: "Hang on a minute. I just realized something! I've been a victim of my own bias."

A bias is a system of judgments we place on the world to simplify complexity. Seeing patterns in behaviors and data helps us come to conclusions faster and make decisions more quickly, but this is often a double-edged sword. These patterns can limit us and others. And at its worst, a bias can be toxic, especially when we aren't aware of it.

Everyone has biases. Everyone. And not just the kind that human resources keeps an eye on. Research suggests that we filter our experiences and inclinations through a range of biases—at least half a dozen daily. Here are a few common individual biases:

- Conformity Bias: Our willingness to adapt our behavior to the crowd.

- Authority Bias: Our tendency to be influenced by those in positions of power.

- Anchoring Bias: Our reliance on the first piece of information we are given on a topic.

- Recency Bias: Our tendency to remember the most recent events or interactions.

- Confirmation Bias: Our tendency to cherry-pick information that confirms our existing views.

My client experienced confirmation bias. They selectively collected information that backed-up opinions about their colleagues. By ascribing colleagues' behavior to malicious intent, when it might have been perfectly innocent, my client created the conditions for a self-fulfilling prophecy: I feel like an outsider, I act like an outsider, so I'm guaranteed to be seen as an outsider.

Becoming aware of our own biases and mitigating their impact isn't easy, particularly the biases you've held—consciously or unconsciously—for a long time. They're comfortable. They can seem effective. They "work" for us. Until they don't. In reality, the problem is never solely with other people. And while bias is a function of us, it's not all about us.

My client's behavior is an example of how easy it is to point out others' faults. We can get caught up in how *we* are being treated; how people are working against *us*; and how others make *our* lives difficult.

If we want to understand and address our own biases, it takes courage, effort, and discomfort. That's why it is rare to intentionally reflect on how we are treating *others*; how we work against *others*; and how we make *others'* lives difficult.

However hard it is to address individual biases, institutional biases are far more difficult to resolve. But you can start with one person: yourself. And in terms of examining individual biases, you can model who you want to be, and shape the world you want to live in, beginning with the following five steps.

STEP 1: Acknowledge that no one is without bias

- To simplify a complex world, we all take mental shortcuts. We willingly adapt our behavior, we can be influenced by certain people or events, and we rely on select information.

- Accepting your own biases without beating yourself up helps you practice grace. It leads to self-awareness and self-acceptance. The truth is, we're all human beings.

STEP 2: Understand how individual biases show up for you and others

- Listen to the way people speak, word choice, and comments—or lack of.

- Observe body language. Stance, gestures, and facial expressions are silent signals. Feel what your body is telling you through signs like a heightened pulse or a sense of unease. How are we acting and how are others responding to us? This is a two-way street.

- Register if others are shutting down or checking out, a tell-tale indicator that there is individual bias in the room. But is it yours? Someone else's?

- Pay attention to your inner running monologue. Who are you silently distrusting, dismissing, or judging? And are you using this information to confirm your existing biases or are you adapting your thoughts?

STEP 3: Don't fill information gaps with negative narratives

- It's difficult not to judge people who you think are judging you.

- Often, assumptions turn out to be false. This may result in comical misunderstandings, but it could have dire consequences.

- With anchoring bias, for example, we rely on the first piece of information we are given on a topic. On day one of a new job, you may have been told that a particular person was hard to get along with. So you avoid them, you don't include them in a team lunch, you don't invite them to be part of an initiative. Months later, you're placed together on a project. You can't believe it, but this person is kind and diligent, easy to get along with. Maybe you'll both laugh about your mistake, but if they don't find it funny, you can miss out on a good relationship with a valuable colleague and, potentially, a friend.

- When in doubt, just ask! "When you said x, what did you mean?" Clarify at the source. Get your own information and come to your own conclusions.

STEP 4: Build commonality

- Reach out.

- Stay curious.

- Establish what you and others have in common, not what is different.

- Focus on what brings people together, not what sets us apart.

- Being more inclusive in our thoughts and actions naturally creates connections.

STEP 5: Focus on you

- This is where you have the most control.

- Be the very best version of yourself. Every day.

Progress is better than perfection. Be better today than you were yesterday, and even better tomorrow. Keep an open mind about a person's ability to show up differently, so they have the opportunity to. (And that includes you.)

MOVING FROM SCARCITY TO SUCCESS TO SIGNIFICANCE

SCARCITY CAN DEFINE our early careers. You don't have a big title, if any. You don't wield much power or influence, and you probably don't make as much money as you'd like. You may have a handful of relationships, the beginnings of a network, but basically, you're just getting your feet wet—just learning the ropes.

Moving from scarcity to success requires a certain amount of struggle. This is true regardless of birth circumstances and upbringing, and whether you've become an entrepreneur, C-level executive, community leader, government agent, military leader, or non-profit head. Different people, different stakes, different struggles. No one is immune.

But struggle is not an outcome; rather it's a pathway on which we build the resilience to evolve and grow. Scientists recently tried growing trees in a biodome setting, but the trees kept falling over. There wasn't any wind pushing against the trees, so they didn't develop a robust root system. For humans, struggle brings learning and meaning that some value even more than their success.

In the working world, your early career struggles may be focused on the following questions:

- How can you deliver results on a consistent basis?

- How can you make your way up to positions of power and influence?

- How can you influence others? What can you do to control, manage, and organize people and the wider organization?

- How can you navigate relationships? How can you build trust?

- How can you grow your impact by promoting yourself and your team?

- What kind of strategic connections can you make or build upon?

So you struggle on. And if you're one of those who can overcome Shakespeare's slings and arrows of outrageous fortune, you may achieve what looks to the outside world like success: a thriving business, a partnership, a fancy company car, a lucrative buyout, those stars on your uniform. Yet an emptiness that's hard to explain can often accompany success.

Your definition of success can be singular and self-focused. In a material world, the acquisition of wealth to buy things like houses, cars, and clothes can easily be mistaken for success. But material things are superficial and temporary. And they don't guarantee joy.

Your identity is wrapped up in success. But often, succeeding once is not enough. You feel pressure to succeed over and over again.

When you accomplish a long-held goal that you define success by—graduating from a top-ranked college, becoming a CEO, owning a second home—you find that past the first champagne-burst of success, you feel flat. It doesn't make you happy the way you thought it would.

Perhaps you had the goal for so long that you don't know what life looks like without it. So now what?

The problem is we think happiness will be on the other side of something great instead of contained within the gritty but rewarding process of getting there. The joy is in the journey.

When the glow of money, power, and status fades, it can be an isolating, disorienting experience. For the reasons above, we can lose our sense of meaning and purpose. To get them back, we can turn our focus toward service.

Reject the constant fixation on your own wants in favor of celebrating others' success by using your platform, resources, network, and time—markers of your own success that you have at your disposal—to give others opportunities to succeed.

These humble acts of service may be the most significant way we can leave our mark on the world because there's a multiplier effect at play. We're only one person, but we can positively impact many people's lives. And in turn, they may be inspired to do great (or greater) things. The net widens, potential grows, change ripples—sustainably, limitlessly.

THE LEADER AS A COMMUNITY BUILDER

THIS SECTION CONSIDERS the team dimension of leadership.

As we touched on in the opening section, every leader should aim to become a *community builder* with like-minded, motivated supporters. That means honing the ability to <u>focus on others</u> as well as developing superior <u>communication</u> skills that create connections.

KEY COMPETENCIES

Communication

Practicing effective communication (verbal/non-verbal/ listening) across various settings (one-on-one, small group, presentations, large groups).

A focus on others

Leaders understand other people's motivations and help them live up to their full potential, both individually and collectively.

IN SHORT

People look to leaders to help them feel connected to the collective, to become a part of something bigger than themselves. Great leaders communicate well, build great teams, develop others, and grow relationships to help people feel *a sense of belonging*.

As you read through the next ten chapters, think about how you show up as a Community Builder. In what ways do you connect with others? How do you make sure people connect within the team? What kind of conditions encourage deeper connections? And how can you elevate those connections to create a sense of belonging?

REDLINING: HOW TO AVOID IT

LEADERS OFTEN DESCRIBE their lives in breathless terms, like they're stuck on a speedway, and charging toward the finish line of a never-ending race. It makes sense. Leaders are responsible for their team's effectiveness, and it's hard not to keep revving up the power and speed.

If a leader is comparable to the car's engine, then the team's capabilities are like a car's gears. Think of gears this way:

- Gears convert the leader's energy into motion. They determine how effectively leadership is translated into action and accomplishment.

- A team with the right gears leverages the leader's energy, helping you to move more quickly, and with less effort.

- If the team has the right gears but they are not being used effectively, then the leader will need to run harder and faster. You'll need to fill in the gaps by increasing your efforts. But even though you are working harder, the results may still be suboptimal.

- Worse, all that extra work will bring the car's engine—you, the leader—closer to the redline.

THE REDLINE

In a car, gears harness the engine's power and transfer it into speed. In high gear, the engine runs comfortably at around 2,500 revolutions per minute (rpm). But to get to the same speed in a lower gear, the engine will run at over 5,000 rpm. This is close to the "redline": the maximum speed the engine can tolerate without causing long-term damage.

Redlining in a car is not sustainable. It's useful in a crisis—to steer away from danger, for example—but if you drive too fast in first gear day in, day out, the engine burns out and gears wear out. Redlining at work isn't sustainable either—leaders stress, good people leave. But we all know why it happens.

In our early careers, we are trained, incentivized, recognized, and rewarded when we focus on accomplishing tasks, solving problems, and getting things done. Our value to the organization, our promotability—sometimes even our identity—are defined by it.

In the middle and late stages of our careers, though, we will typically take on senior leadership roles where we're supposed to guide our team to accomplish those tasks.

Supposed to.

It's hard to stop revving your engine when you've always been task oriented. It's hard to rely on others. But to avoid redlining, you must shift gears.

SHIFTING GEARS

It's impossible to shift gears without incorporating time into your schedule for strategic reflection. That's a given. The biggest key to operating at a higher level with less effort, however, is the strength of your gears. Here are a few questions to ask about your team's capabilities:

- How can you use your current gears more effectively?

- How can you use the team's capabilities to translate your energy into action?

- Can you add more gears to your gearbox?

- When is the best time to upgrade the gearbox? How?

Once you evaluate, modify, and develop the individual and collective skills of the team... start to delegate. And then delegate some more. You'll work faster and more productively without burning out the engine (that's you) or wearing down your gears (the team). You'll speed up the journey, but instead of redlining, you can cruise along at a fast but sustainable pace. And even, enjoy the ride!

FEAR IS A SHORT-TERM MOTIVATOR

T HERE ARE TWO kinds of leaders: those who trust their team members and those who generate fear in them. You've probably worked for both. We tend to remember emotionally extreme experiences—positive or negative—so you are likely to have fond memories about the leaders who believed in you, but distinctly different feelings about the ones who didn't.

Reflect on your time working for those two types of leaders. Ask yourself:

- How did they impact your motivation level?

- How did they change the way you worked back then?

- How are those experiences still affecting you now?

FEAR

The fear created by a crisis can squeeze out the best in you at work. Fear may help you push through a deadline or deal with an emergency such as a line going down, a quality mistake, a PR disaster, or a client catastrophe. In these specific, often critical moments, you tend to react instinctively. Your focus narrows on the danger in front of you. Your energy contracts. You get dragged into the tactical details of the immediate moment.

But having a leader who works through fear on top of the fear produced by a crisis—or just in the challenges of the day-to-day operations—makes things much worse.

Fear is a short-term motivator. Spiked cortisol levels, adrenaline rushes, an increased heart rate, operating in flight or fight mode—none of it is sustainable. Besides wrecking your peripheral vision, fear-based thinking and behavior clouds perspective and judgment. You feel stressed, pressured, drained.

TRUST

To achieve long-term growth and success with their teams, leaders should communicate a different emotion: love. Trust is the work expression of love. Essentially, when a leader trusts, they're saying: I support you and I accept you;

I believe you will do the best you can with the resources at your disposal.

Fear is easy. It is instinctive. And it gets your attention. But it is a contracting force.

Trust is hard. It takes courage. And it takes effort. But it is an expansive force—and an important long-term motivator. When you work with a leader who trusts you, you can relax into your role and focus on the tasks at hand. You can create your best work.

GETTING THE BEST OUT OF TEAMS

Emergencies happen and being able to decipher and differentiate genuine threats from perceived ones—that's one of a leader's most critical jobs. But true emergencies are also rare. And the finest leaders, those who are skilled at getting the best out of their teams by discerning between the immediate and the important:

- Respond instead of reacting.

- Are willing and able to provide air cover to remove pressure in the working environment.

- Protect their team's energy to stop them from feeling overly drained.

There are two competing forces in the world: fear and love (or trust). The way a leader shows up communicates whether they prioritize one or the other.

Working without any fear at all can lead to complacency and mediocrity within the team. Without trust, the working environment is unforgiving and unsustainable. But as the saying goes, a head full of fears has no space for dreams. And when leaders make their teams feel trusted rather than uncertain and afraid, they make room for them to thrive.

MAKE YOURSELF
REDUNDANT

SKILLED MANAGERS—OR GOOD leaders—are responsible for understanding their team's resources and developing their capabilities, culture, and resilience. They tend to direct and drive decision-making from the center of the action.

But once a team is strong and capable, with a robust and thriving culture, *great* leaders know how to step away from the center and let their team figure out how to succeed on their own. In other words, great leaders make themselves redundant.

MAKE YOURSELF
REDUNDANT

The truth is, leadership is never a one-person show, because without a team, even the most talented person can only be an individual contributor. Still, the idea of working yourself out of a job is a tough ask, difficult to grasp in both theory and practice. Like most people, leaders want to be seen providing value, not as someone who is irrelevant or who no longer contributes. It's an existential conundrum.

But when leaders build a sustainable, high-performing, autonomous team with built-in successors—when they intentionally make themselves redundant—typically none of those fears materialize. Instead, leaders often obtain greater success with fewer direct inputs, an increase in scope and responsibility, and maybe even a promotion.

And here's why.

In business, "gravity" can pull leaders into the organization's weeds, leaving them stuck focusing on tasks below their level, bogged down by the day-to-day grind. There's a "weightlessness" to making yourself redundant. Letting the team take care of the day-to-day work while you explore the bigger picture? It's freeing.

The leader will be able to integrate those tactical activities at an enterprise-level in accordance with the strategic direction. When they hand over day-to-day tasks to the team, they're free to ensure that work is integrated with enterprise-level strategy. They'll also have time to reflect on their own contributions to the company. For example: What's the mood across the organization, among my peers and peer-level colleagues? How are my communications flowing up and down the organization?

Plus, a leader with the confidence to let their team off-leash has the mental space to evaluate what is happening—and what might happen—outside the organization: customers, competitors, technology, industry trends, macro factors.

The team benefits, too, if they are working at the appropriate level. Feeling confident and comfortable leads to growth in the form of additional experience and exposure to the wider organization.

HOW TO BUILD A TEAM THAT CAN LIVE WITHOUT YOU

If a leader is always the hub of their team, then every decision flows through them. A lot of spokes, a lot of tasks, a lot of work. To get unstuck from this central—obstructive—position, develop the team and get out of the way. The leader can begin by doing a triage on incoming requests from the team or the organization through asking these questions:

- *Is it truly important?* If not, figure out how the team can handle it.

- *Is it mine to solve?* If not, appoint someone else to do it.

- *Does it need to be solved right now?* If not, it can wait until later. Take time to come up with a strategic plan of action.

- *Is there anyone else who can help?* If so... get those people involved!

The issue may need the leader's assistance. And in that case, they should determine how best to involve the team. There might even be a way to offer the team a stretch challenge. Just make sure it requires less, little—or no—input from the leader themselves.

Making yourself redundant might feel uncomfortable at first, but keeping two things in mind might give you some relief:

1. So many good things lie on the other side of discomfort.

2. Unless you change your approach, you'll get the same results and stay bogged down in details well below your ability and pay grade.

Courage, planning, confidence, and self-belief. Faith in yourself and faith in your team. Making yourself redundant takes all of these. But most of all, it requires a shift in perspective. Leaders are not handing off tasks so that they have none; they are building a bench of talent that will support, replace, and, one day (maybe) surpass them. Bringing out the greatness in others—that's what great leaders do.

FRONTLOADING

"I don't run my calendar; my calendar runs me."

A FULL WEEK OF obligations lined up by Monday morning. Unplanned crises. Little room for breaks, perspective, and reflection. For leaders who are often rendered powerless by it, overplanned time can be a silent drag on their energy. And ultimately, their effectiveness.

STANDARD PROJECT MANAGEMENT

Figure 3 shows how time can impact a leader's energy throughout the typical stages of a project.

FIGURE 3: STANDARD PROJECT MANAGEMENT—TIME AND ENERGY EXPENDITURE

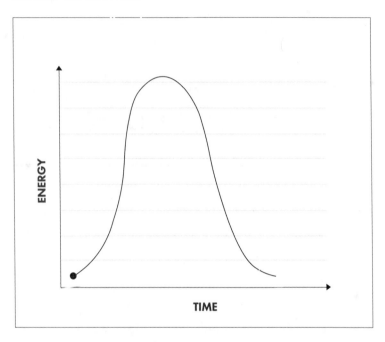

Initial kickoff meeting held

- The leader outlines the big picture for the team. For example: project goals, timeline, responsibilities, resources, and constraints.

- The leader confirms consensus with the team and the project is launched.

- In this stage, the leader's time commitment is low—perhaps two to three hours—and their energy expenditure is low, as well.

Then something happens!

- A client changes their request. Project requirements shift. Competitors make a move that alters the market. Any of these will drive a project off target—as will a material delay or a supplier slip-up, or even a mistake inside your own team.

- In this stage, the leader's time commitment is at a medium level… and growing. Because they have to bring more focus to what is going on (or going wrong!), the leader's energy expenditure is also at a medium.

The leader plays detective

- Now, the project's mission is threatened. Derailment can occur for an hour, a day, a week, a month, or several months. And it grabs everyone's time and attention.

- Tensions rise and tempers shorten—by the minute. Amid this stressful environment, the leader must figure out what happened.

- The leader may resent being sucked back into the project in such detail. Not only is time lost but trust as well, as team members try to shift blame, and the leader has to figure out who's telling the truth.

- Team members may also feel on edge, especially those who must complete their daily tasks on top of dealing with new problems.

- At this stage, the leader is fully engaged. Both their time commitment and energy expenditure are high.

The project gets back on track

- Following a grand inquiry, emergency meetings, detailed analysis, email tornados, and maybe late nights, the project gets back on track.

- The team may feel anxiety around changes and increased workloads. Trust between leader and team—and among team members—can continue to decrease.

- The stress isn't over. The leader is busy mitigating the consequences of the derailment, so their time commitment and energy expenditure remains high.

The project nears completion

- As hysteria fades and the storm softens, team members get back to work based on the new direction. But consequences like hidden psychological wounds and lowered opinions of their colleagues often remain.

- The leader's time commitment and energy expenditure return to lower levels.

FRONTLOADING

There's an old boxing adage: Everyone has a plan until they get punched in the face. That's why you need more than one plan. Starting with several backup plans, each with built-in contingencies for various scenarios—which should include "if we get punched in the face"—gives you a chance to survive the first strike. It's called frontloading.

Frontloading requires putting more leader-run team activities at the beginning of a process to prevent chaos in the middle. Frontloading can be effective for short-term project management as well as longer-term strategic leadership.

Figure 4 demonstrates how frontloading both the team's and the leader's activities can help mitigate the effects of time-busting and energy-depleting issues. It's a different approach that anticipates uncertainty to create the conditions for success.

FIGURE 4: FRONTLOADED PROJECT MANAGEMENT—TIME AND
ENERGY EXPENDITURE

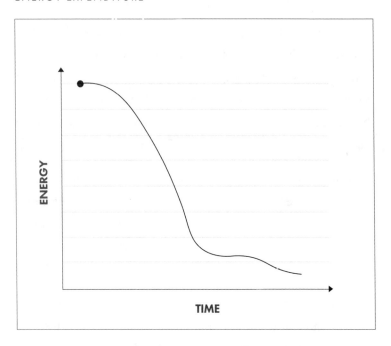

Initial kickoff meetings held

- Instead of one big meeting, multiple meetings are held. These may be spread over several days and weeks.

- The leader works with the team on scenario and contingency planning. The leader doesn't "push" expectations and actions onto the team; they "pull" ideas from the team. They may ask, for instance: What are the pressing issues? What could derail the process? Are there weaknesses within the plan and if so, how can they be mitigated on the front end?

- The leader, who is busy facilitating resilience, foresight, and transparency among the team, is highly involved. They're finding out answers to questions like: What happens if customer requirements change? Is there flexibility—externally with clients and providers or internally within our own processes? How will we know if we are off track?

- The team may have difficult conversations about issues like timelines, resources, capabilities, or limitations. But talking through these details before a project starts helps everyone figure out solutions before problems arise.

- The leader confirms consensus with the team and the project is launched.

- The leader's time commitment and energy expenditure are both high in this period. But these efforts are in service of better planning on the front end—which will save time and energy downstream for everyone involved.

Manageable interruptions

- After the initial kickoff meetings, the leader's time commitment and energy expenditure will steadily decrease until the project is complete.

- At some point, there will be an issue. This is depicted by a bump in the graph. But the leader and the team have (over) prepared and (over) planned at the beginning of a project. They have developed alternative scenarios and contingencies, so they won't have to revisit and correct as many problems. And if problems do surface, they are manageable.

In a fast-paced environment, most leaders don't plan adequately because they "don't have enough time." But ironically, what often keeps them from having time is dealing with the fallout from lack of planning on a previous project.

Frontloading breaks this cycle. When a leader intentionally spends time where it is best served—before a project launches—they won't have to deal with crisis after crisis in an emotionally heightened state. They'll save time and energy down the road. They'll be spared the figurative punch in the face.

THE STRUCTURE
TO GROW

A LEADER SHARES SOME of the same qualities as a gardener. To begin with, both occupations require practice. You simply cannot become a leader or a gardener—especially a good one—overnight. Reading manuals and learning from experts is certainly important, but when you roll up your sleeves and get your hands dirty, those learnings may be even richer and deeper rooted.

Both jobs also require patience—and plenty of it. A successful team that's made up of robust, colorful, and thriving members is like a garden full of flourishing plants, and neither happens immediately. They require time and tending to grow. Besides waiting (and waiting and waiting and waiting), there's ongoing testing to determine what's working best. There's also lots of trial and error, figuring it out, adaptation.

And flexibility.

A flexible plan might be the most important component in building a great garden or a great team. And when that flexibility is surrounded by a sturdy, protective framework, there's even more growth potential. Plants, like people, need both freedom and structure. They need something to support them, something solid they can push back against as they learn to stand on their own during each stage of the growing cycle. Providing that strong, steady support is a leader's role in the workplace.

In addition, just like a gardener, a leader has many tasks. Let's explore a few of them.

PLANTING

Planting is adding capable people to the team—and *capable* comes in all different varieties! For example, some team members may be like cactuses, who don't require much attention and can thrive without a lot of resources. Others may be orchids, who need lots of attention but will produce an abundance of stunning flowers.

In this most foundational stage, the leader can have several jobs:

- Understanding what (or who) will thrive in the working environment. Gardens have areas of sunshine and shade. So do teams. Some plants love the sunshine while others like to hide out in the shade, and it's about being aware of how different people respond to different conditions.

- Knowing how to select a variety of complementary plants, with diversity that's seen and unseen. Including lots of different plants makes for a beautiful, more resilient, layered—fruitful—garden.

- Realizing when it's time to evolve or expand the team. It's important to dig out the members who are not growing so there's room for those who are. Making sure that these and any other new plants complement the existing ones is essential.

WATERING

For a leader, "watering" their team means making sure team members get the daily nourishment of feedback and communication—it's ongoing. A heavier watering is required for difficult challenges. This might take more of a leader's time, but only with such thorough support and guidance do team members grow.

FERTILIZING

To accelerate growth, the leader will feed their team stretch opportunities, challenges, training, and coaching. Cross-functional initiatives—like a new product launch or an IT implementation—are also vital to the mix because they expose team members to experiences outside of the team or function. When implemented with care and forethought, this intentional broadening often helps to quicken expansion in an individual's skillset or mindset.

PRUNING

We all know what pruning means. And it happens when a leader trims the scope of a team member who has overgrown their boundaries to help them focus their energy on developing a thicker core—while ignoring what's not central.

WEEDING

Inspirational speaker Alexander den Heijer said: "When a flower doesn't bloom you fix the environment in which it grows, not the flower." A leader weeds when they identify obstacles (sometimes even other team members) that inhibit individual success—whether that is unnecessary bureaucracy or paralyzed decision-making—and then eliminates them.

GREEN THUMBS

Leaders and gardeners can develop a gift for growing if they practice, and practice patiently and attentively, within a flexible plan. And when the hard work is done, the beautiful, more resilient, layered—fruitful—harvest they'll reap will make all that planting, watering, fertilizing, pruning, and weeding worthwhile.

PERFORM, PREPARE, RECOVER

SUCCESSFUL ATHLETES AND highly trained military operatives balance performance, preparation, and recovery to stay at the top of their game. Yet many leaders would consider such a regimen impossible—perhaps laughable. Most leaders spend an overriding majority of their working life in "performance mode." But this dramatic imbalance, with little or no time spent on preparation and recovery, has severe spill-over consequences.

When you as a leader don't sufficiently prepare—for example, setting expectations, outcomes, and rules of engagement, or creating a clear playbook for crisis management—you won't be ready to perform. And you won't be able to help your team perform to the best of their ability. Without a prepared leader, team members will lack agility, flexibility, resilience, and ultimately, autonomy.

Internal systems can become fragile, and people can feel confused and directionless.

If you don't leave time for yourself to recover, the stress will drain you. Whether you're conscious of it or not, as the leader, you will lose energy and perspective. A leader's exhaustion affects the team just as much as their own burnout, and in the end, team members will assume, or become a recipient of, your stress. Team members won't recover, either, and those deficiencies drain the team's spirit, connectedness, and focus.

When leaders bring balance to performance, preparation, and recovery, they, too, can stay at the top of their game. It's not about perfectly balancing these three areas equally. That's both unrealistic and unnecessary. A more sustainable, strategic ratio might be: 60% perform + 30% prepare + 10% recovery.

In a fifty-hour work week, that looks like thirty hours of performing, fifteen hours of preparation (note that unlike athletes, leaders need to prepare not just themselves, but their team, so these hours need to be split up among self-development and team development), and five hours of recovery.

PERFORM

Performance is action-based. It may include a client presentation, a kickoff meeting for a new project, a town hall—anything that directly moves the business forward. These situations are typically stressful. Perhaps you must deliver a complex presentation, solve a pressing problem, justify a decision, explain why something (typically something "bad") happened, or provide an update on a project.

To reduce their own performance hours, the leader can:

- Simplify communications. Only review or present what is necessary—and do it at the appropriate time. For example, don't react instantly to every new email.

- Prioritize actions. Stick to what's mission-critical and/or value-added—the rest can wait!

To increase performance hours for their team, the leader can:

- Share the load. When others take the lead, they learn and develop skills. Plus, it gives you more time to prepare and recover!

PREPARE

Preparation evolves the leader and the team's skills and resilience—along with associated systems and processes—that contribute to long-term success. It can be self-development or team development, formal or informal.

To increase their own preparation hours, the leader can:

- Make sense of a recent issue and take the time to apply learnings—before starting the work, throughout the process, and once the work is done. Like the saying goes... the more you know!

- Get ready for a board meeting, a quarterly business review, or a client interaction. You'll be cooler, calmer, and more collected.

To increase preparation hours for their team, the leader can:

- Support direct reports, as needed, for an upcoming event. Do they have sufficient resources? Are timelines and objectives clear?

- Empower team members. Let them take on an initiative. Give them broader exposure to other functions in the organization.

- Give the team stretch goals. While mitigating organizational risk, push members to do things that challenge them.

- Coach the team on what's important. Communicate levers for success and reinforce how the team will work together to achieve them.

RECOVER

Recovery is restorative. It includes activities like noodling, reading, strategic thinking, "recharging batteries," and celebrating wins with the team. While it is important to create the space to experience these recovery moments within the work week—and not just outside of it, during evenings and weekends—sometimes this may be more of an aspiration than a possibility.

To increase their own recovery hours, the leader can:

- Spend at least an hour a day staring out of the window. (Yes, really.) Looking at information from a different perspective helps to discover patterns that others can't see.

- Actively reflect. This may be as simple as allowing the past day's events to sink in. What was learned? Who needs to know? How can the team make the business better tomorrow, as a result?

- Leave the schedule open for an intentional moment (or two) to think about the future. This helps to anticipate and prepare for unforeseen or unexpected challenges.

To increase recovery hours for their team, the leader can:

- Celebrate with the team. Appreciation builds connection and community. It gives the team shared experiences of success that build the foundation of trust, acknowledgement, and camaraderie.

- Give the team time off. Even short breaks can be restorative. In the long run, rest leads to increased energy and motivation.

When leaders bring balance to performance, preparation, and recovery, they stay at the top of their game so they can bring out the best in their team, too. Everyone wins. That's thirty hours of performing, fifteen hours of preparation, and five hours of recovery. Think about your week... are you anywhere close to this? If not, what will you do?

WHEN YOU SPEED,
YOU LOSE

I N OUR FAST-PACED, information-heavy, results-driven world, it can feel like we're always moving quickly. Oftentimes, we may even worry that we're not moving quickly enough. And while it may be energizing to travel at the speed of life, there are downsides.

The inattention that comes from racing through your day can cause a range of organizational consequences. You can believe it's easier and more efficient to do the work yourself rather than letting others learn or give it a try. If you're constantly speeding, you can lose three critical leadership skills: prioritization, communication, and delegation.

If you don't slow down to <u>prioritize</u> tasks and objectives, for example:

- You can feel overwhelmed. "We need everything, yesterday. Twice!" If nothing is a priority, then everything is.

- You risk directing your team's energy toward non-value-added efforts. If you don't clarify priorities for your team, you can easily and inadvertently create chaos. It's highly inefficient, at best.

- You can get bogged down in the details of a certain task at the expense of others. Without allocating time and energy to the right areas, you and your team could get stuck in the weeds.

- Without clear direction, your team can become *unfocused*.

If communication gets lost in the race for action:

- You can miss updates. This may leave certain team members being uninformed or feeling left out.

- You can create information gaps when data and/or the context is missing and/or inaccurate. Others may fill in these gaps with irrelevant details or incorrect narratives, which undermine team alignment.

- You can miss opportunities to make sure the team understands the big picture. How the pieces of a project fit together or how effectively the team is managing overall objectives, for instance.

- With team members operating on different sets of information, many of them without seeing the bigger picture, your team can become *disjointed*.

Why should you entrust a task to others that you can do easily? Because it doesn't hurt—in most cases the job will be done just as well—and you can focus on more important work. On the other hand, if you don't <u>delegate</u>:

- You can inadvertently become a bottleneck to team and organizational success. If you're asking too much of yourself, your workload will ultimately become overwhelming, even impossible to accomplish in a timely manner.

- How can you expect the team to ever learn? And if team members don't learn, you'll always be stuck doing the work… and resenting it.

- You won't be able to leverage downtime when things are slower. Without reflection, our actions are simply stand-alone tasks—and we lose the bigger lessons around success or failure.

- When things really do get busy, you will struggle to break this restrictive pattern of behavior. And if the team breaks down because of this—taking on unfamiliar tasks under pressure, unaware of the bigger picture—it's the leader's fault. And the leader's fault alone.

- Without chances to learn and develop their autonomy because you won't delegate, your team can become *constrained*.

DON'T HESITATE, DELEGATE!

Of these three important leadership skills—prioritizing, communicating, and delegation—delegation is the most closely linked to community building. It's the best method for leaders to leverage their available resources in the seemingly constant fight against time. It's tricky to get it right sometimes, though, because there's a spectrum of trust involved—micromanaging at one end and abdication at the other, with delegation somewhere in the middle.

Micromanaging is when a leader attempts to control every last detail of a task, regardless of its size or importance. It can be annoying. It can make people feel untrusted. And when micromanaging becomes too suffocating, people often quit.

Abdication is when a leader assigns tasks without providing context, resources, objectives, milestones, and support. It's sort of like throwing the car keys to a new driver and saying, "Good luck, kid." Abdicating responsibility gives people an unjustified amount of trust that results in dangerous overconfidence. It sets them up to fail.

Delegation is when you as the leader trust the team to try out different, and sometimes unfamiliar, activities with your guided support. It's like having the leader sit alongside that same new driver, sharing knowledge, experience, and perspective while also providing help.

Great leaders delegate by having presence without actually being present. How? By declaring, coaching, and reinforcing the framework for decision-making—essentially, sharing the rules of the road. So what effective delegation ultimately means, is that, over time, you can confidently and quietly sit in the back seat and safely enjoy the ride. Maybe your job will be to read the map so you can give the team clear directions. Or perhaps you'll eventually feel comfortable enough to look out the window and dream about where to go next.

UNDERSTANDING THE ROOTS OF CONFLICT

EVERY INDIVIDUAL INTERPRETS and interacts with the world differently. Simply put, people aren't all motivated by the same things. It might seem obvious to say it, but we don't always act like it's true. Misunderstood motivations can be frustrating for everyone and can cause conflict—lots of it. There are three roots of conflict within the workplace: ideological, contextual, and stylistic.

IDEOLOGICAL

Ideologies are deeply held ideas, viewpoints, and principles. Essentially, our rules for living. They can be as profound as religious, political, and spiritual beliefs, or as simple as a preference in working hours or organizational culture. We hold these beliefs closely. And we tend to judge others who don't share them—often harshly.

If leaders refrain from thinking that one ideology is "better" than another, they can create opportunities for the team to celebrate those differences. Being able to see, adapt, and mediate differences may even help the leader unlock challenging team dynamics or solve complex problems. And the team will be better—and work better together—because of it.

If there's ideological conflict within the team, tools for resolution include:

- Persuasion: At a minimum, ask team members to "disagree and commit" to working together. Ideally, get the team to find common ground.

- Compromise: To get consensus for the wider benefit of the organization, find solutions where everyone makes concessions. A sign of a good negotiation is when all parties are a little unhappy!

CONTEXTUAL

A contextual difference occurs when the context, and the roles within it, set people at odds with each other.

In the organization, each team member represents a position, a function, or a group with specific interests and goals. Limited resources can be fought over—even when those parties are organizationally on the same team! Two peers could be friends outside of work and see the world similarly, but put them in different functions where they are competing for scarce internal resources? All hell can break loose.

Conflict may arise in budget cycles or in the strategic planning process, for example, but just as often they crop up in the daily internecine battles for prestige, resources, power, favor, and acknowledgement.

If there's contextual conflict within the team, tools for resolution include:

- Committing to the wider organization: Remind colleagues they are on the same team. Reassure them that there is a solution out there that's acceptable to (nearly!) everyone.

- Adopting a transactional approach: Agree to "quid pro quos." To get team members to accept positive exchanges, the leader may act as a broker, organizing tit-for-tats that benefit the larger organization.

- Zooming out: To solve resource-constrained challenges, encourage team members to expand their perspective. When thinking is open, issues tend to be solved at an enterprise—rather than a functional—level.

STYLISTIC

While someone's style can be affected by an underlying ideology or the contextual specifics, it is typically driven by their preferences and predispositions. Stylistic differences explain the way we work. For example, a person's communication style may be loud and direct versus quiet and subtle; an approach to deadlines may be well organized versus pressure prompted; a management tactic may be prescriptive versus hands-off.

Psychometric assessments capture these personal preferences and predispositions. Using assessments and other tools of self-discovery helps leaders and team members better understand themselves.

Stylistic differences, when correctly handled, can contribute to the team's collective knowledge, wisdom, experience, and expertise. So crafting a path that leverages those differences is a critical job for a leader. Another critical job: managing the team's stylistic differences before they are managed by those differences.

If there's stylistic conflict within the team, tools for resolution include:

- Developing self-awareness: This applies to the leader and the team. We can better understand why and what we dislike when we understand why we are the way we are!

- Remaining calm: When the leader doesn't get triggered—or emotionally highjacked—by conflict between team members, it leads to higher levels of trust and increased engagement.

- Finding alternative approaches: The leader can leverage the best bits of the team's complementary approaches, perspectives, or styles to provide a superior solution.

For team members, being seen and valued is important: so important. It's the foundation of respect and trust. When you as the leader learn about team members' motivations, you're taking a purposeful step toward understanding the potential roots of conflict. And as you then address those individual differences, you create a team that accomplishes more—a team that's worth more than the sum of its parts. It's cliché but it's true... we are better together.

PERFORMANCE PLUS: THE POWER OF TEAMS

NEARLY ALL TEAMS lean in one of two directions. A "results-only" team is driven but it lacks connection and camaraderie. And good relationships are critical, especially during challenging times. A "relationship-only" team is connected, and often compassionate about inclusion and culture, but it lacks results. And the fact is that without a positive bottom line, there is no team.

CAPABILITY

At work, a capability is the capacity to complete a task. Requisites include intelligence, training, and/or experience.

When a leader evaluates the capabilities of a team or team member, they might ask these questions:

- Is there sufficient capability to run day-to-day activities? Or are there gaps in skills, experience, staff, or training?

- Does the person or team deal with conflict constructively? If there is disagreement among members, can they resolve the issue and implement a solution without outside direction, mediation, or guidance?

- How well does the person or team operate autonomously? Can they solve external issues through agility, flexibility, intelligence, and resilience?

MOTIVATION

Motivation relates not only to a team member's willingness to commit to action, but also to put the team or the organization's goals alongside or ahead of their own. When a leader evaluates the motivations of a team or team member, they might ask these questions:

- Is the person or team committed to the organization's goals and determined to do what it takes to achieve them?

- Does the person or team collaborate and communicate effectively? Do team members genuinely care for each other?

- Do team members lean on and learn from each other?

PERFORMANCE PLUS

Obviously, results are central to success. But leaders who can balance a task-focus with a people-focus can take the team's performance to the next level. A team that is sustainable and high achieving with a blend of collaboration and reliable results—that's "Performance Plus."

Figure 5 demonstrates a team's capability and motivation. The first step in giving your team the right balance of task-focus and a people-focus, is to think about where on this graph every team member falls.

FIGURE 5: CAPABILITY AND MOTIVATION—A LEADER'S ACTIONS

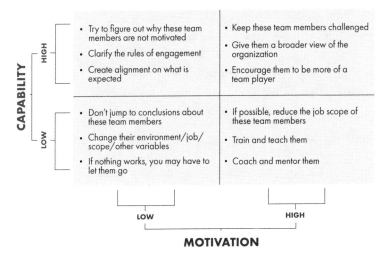

In identifying each team member's capability and motivation, the leader's objective is also to understand the limitations of their team. Based on this evaluation, you can help individual team members improve—and create the conditions for the team to level-up to Performance Plus.

The following is a brief description of how the people in each quadrant might show up, along with suggested ways you can help them improve.

The top-right quadrant

Capability: High.

Motivation: High.

These individuals don't need much direct supervision. You can communicate the team's goals, agree on a check-in date... and then get out the way, knowing those team members will be back if they need anything.

Leaders might think that stacking the team with highly capable and highly motivated employees will yield consistently high-performance levels. But that's a mistake because the top-right quadrant is populated by two types.

The Type-A people are extremely capable, but their motivation is to make *themselves* look good; these people can be critical of others and may be gunning for the leader's job and not afraid to say it! The other types are just as capable, but they are highly motivated to make the *team* look good. It's your job to spot the difference.

It's natural for A-types to stand up and lead. You can teach them about the importance of teamwork and how to bring out the best in their peers—and help them recognize when it's better to stand down and follow.

The bottom-left quadrant

Capability: Low.

Motivation: Low.

You might think the answer is to cull those with limited capabilities and low motivation (unwillingness to positively contribute to the team or organization). And oftentimes, that's right. But a mistake many leaders make is to overlook how people, circumstances, and, even, themselves, may have contributed to a team member becoming unmotivated or overwhelmed.

Behavior is communication. Consider that sometimes, team members may simply need more attention, another perspective, or just old-fashioned encouragement and patience. Changes in scope, resources, relationships between team members, or short-term flexibility to deal with a personal issue, are all within your control. If you take time to understand why someone is behaving a certain way, you can change the variables to create a different, and probably better, outcome.

The top-left quadrant

Capability: High.

Motivation: Low.

Clarity and communication are critical in helping these individuals increase their motivation level. This also applies to the top-left quadrant group.

You should meet with these team members in a one-on-one setting, where there is little opportunity for distraction, to figure out what is getting in the way of their being a team player. Clarifying the team's rules of engagement is key. The second step is identifying relationship issues and unpacking team dynamics, because if they're not aligned with the other team members, these people can singlehandedly destroy teamwork.

The bottom-right quadrant

Capability: Low.

Motivation: High.

Formal training, cross-functional learning, or informal mentoring can help these enthusiastic, heart-of-the-team individuals develop their skills. Sometimes reducing the scope of the role can get them back on track. Regular check-ins to measure progress and celebrate growth will likely contribute to their self-confidence.

When you blend your team members' capabilities and motivation, you get a team that's more than the sum of its parts—a high achieving team that can withstand disruption, change, and initiative shifts while continuing to deliver results. That's "Performance Plus." And that's powerful.

SIX STEPS FOR
A HAPPY LIFE

PEOPLE OFTEN TELL themselves that when they become successful, they will be happy. But the opposite is often true. Behind the scenes, many business professionals who have the outer trappings of success—C-suite executives, partners, business owners, entrepreneurs—don't consider themselves particularly happy. Some, not at all.

Success is more likely to be a by-product of happiness than the other way around; in any case, they may overlap, but they are not the same. And of course, no person is happy all the time.

You can be successful AND happy, though. And these special leaders tend to possess six characteristics that contribute to their joyful appreciation of the world:

#1: Stable roots

Stable roots doesn't mean "coming from a perfect childhood." (Spoiler alert: No one's was.) Nor does it mean your present life pie is balanced with equal slices of work, health, spirituality, money, relationships, and fun. (Spoiler alert: No one's is.)

Instead, stable roots are connected to two personal characteristics: self-awareness—knowing who you are—and a consistently calm and values-centered temperament. These qualities contribute to an unflappable sense of self: a self that isn't shaken by challenging circumstances or overwhelmed by life's inevitable ups and downs; a self whose steadiness inspires others.

Aim: (Inspire) others.

#2: A focus on helping others win

Winning signifies success. You win. You look good. You feel good. You're rewarded. Repeat.

When you help others, it's a different emotion—something more like profound well-being. Moving beyond yourself to inspire and motivate others to live up to their fullest potential gives you the opportunity to create, contribute to, and feel part of something bigger. It impacts the wider world. It nourishes a sense of belonging, for you and others.

Aim: (Nourish) others.

#3: Guiding principles

The world can be an unpredictable place. The only constant is change, right?

But you can simplify and codify complexity in meaningful ways—by capturing thoughts and insights about the world, by anticipating change, and by identifying invisible forces, universal laws, and patterns—to understand why things happen. A framework that makes uncertain events and subtle dynamics more manageable creates an organized sense of meaning. When that framework is shared with your team, it helps them to be efficient, successful, and focused.

Aim: (Organize) others.

#4: Passion

Anyone can imagine a better world. But inspiring individuals are not just dreamers. They're able to create—and communicate, through their words and their actions—a clear sense of purpose.

When you are passionate about the change you want to see in the world, it's contagious. Your positive energy spills over. It motivates others to be a part of something they could not have accomplished alone.

Aim: (Motivate) others.

#5: The ability to put wins and losses into perspective

Having a sense of perspective is both grounding and centering. When you're grounded, you have a cheerful humility. You are aware of your limitations and also recognize that you can still impact the world in positive ways—and then you focus on the actions you *can* take. When you're centered, you get that there are people better off and worse off than you, always.

Having a sense of perspective isn't demotivating—it's liberating. Instead of worrying, you can focus on being your best self. Right here, right now. You can take the rough with the smooth. And perspective keeps you from making the same mistakes repeatedly. Instead, you ask questions about your experiences. The answers often turn into information, the information into knowledge, and the knowledge into wisdom that teaches others.

Aim: (Teach) others.

#6: Self-effacing sense of humor

Being able to laugh at yourself and find lightheartedness in challenging situations affirms our shared human experience. When you don't take yourself too seriously, you're practicing humility, and a strong sense of humor can diffuse tension throughout the whole room. Laughing at yourself and acting playful can also connect others, even in the darkest of times.

Aim: (Connect) others.

CREATE THE CONDITIONS FOR HAPPINESS

These six characteristics provide the foundation for a leader's sense of happiness, out of which grows their success. But when you break it down even further, beyond the related actions—inspire, nourish, organize, motivate, teach, connect—it's really all about serving others. Bringing out the best in those around you, that's a true mark of a successful, a happy—a great—leader.

THE LEADER AS A SENSE MAKER

Intelligence
Learning Orientation
SENSE MAKER

THIS SECTION CONSIDERS the context dimension of leadership.

As we touched on in the opening section, this critical sense-making role makes high cognitive/social/emotional intelligence essential for a leader. Great business, social, political, and community leaders also possess a learning orientation that allows them to become *sense makers* during times of change.

KEY COMPETENCIES

Intelligence

Exhibiting higher levels of cognitive, social, and emotional intelligence and using those skills to create meaning for themselves and others.

A learning orientation

An inclination toward curiosity and open-mindedness is a must for leaders to grow themselves, the team, and the organization.

IN SHORT

People want leaders to help them understand and interpret the world. People need leaders to simplify complexity and ease decision-making, and a leader must bring perspective and sound judgment to that task. They learn through others and make sense of information to provide people with a greater *sense of meaning*.

As you read through the next ten chapters, think about how you show up as a Sense Maker. How can you help others understand and interpret the world? In what ways will you improve people's sense of meaning?

THE VIEW FROM
THE INSIDE-OUT AND
THE OUTSIDE-IN

I F YOU WANT to be a great leader, you should spend at least an hour a day—yes, at least an hour—staring out of the window. For any time-starved leader this may sound like an impossible ask, but giving your brain a break lets you process recent events, which creates the conditions for innovative problem-solving.

Patterns, themes, and trends emerge when the brain thinks in a non-linear way. Alternative, innovative solutions might surface, too, because you're not thinking side-to-side or from point A to point B; you're thinking laterally—creatively.

Building intentional gaps for reflection into the day will give you time to digest what's already happened and help you prepare for what may come next.

Still, in a metaphorical sense, your view from inside, looking out the window, has some limits. Let's look at what those limits are—and see how you might overcome them by standing outside that same window, looking in.

THE VIEW FROM THE INSIDE-OUT

What can you see from the inside? First, you see your surroundings. In a work context, that's you, your team, and your organization. These surroundings make up the landscape in which most of your decisions take place. And while it's great to understand that landscape, to feel comfortable within it, this view has drawbacks when it's all you see.

From the inside, your range of vision to the outside is constrained by a narrow window. It's a limited perspective, and this means you—and as a result, your team and your organization—may not see the larger forces at play in the world around you. Macroeconomics, evolving client needs, competitor product launches, industry developments, and changes in the working environment are just a few examples.

You make your decisions, and then your decisions make you. If your frame of reference is restricted, you'll be making decisions based only on what's in your immediate vicinity.

THE VIEW FROM THE OUTSIDE-IN

Imagine standing outside your building and looking at your window. What can you see from the outside? Maybe now your window seems different, perhaps just a small part of the larger panoramic landscape. From out here, you can look right and left—*really* right and left; up and down. Beyond, even.

An important part of being a leader is seeing the bigger picture by looking in all directions. This outside-in view can help you collaborate, communicate, and collect useful information. Here's how:

- Collaboration is left and right, across the organization, at the peer level. You'll be benchmarking activities between functions, offering proactive support to colleagues, and working together on high-level activities.

- Communication is up and down the organization among different levels. You'll be improving communication, providing upward and downward feedback, and ensuring that tactics are consistently tied to the organization's strategic direction.

- Collecting information from outside the organization from clients, end-users, competitors, macroeconomic factors, technology, and industry trends. You'll be bringing this important information inside, to get your team and the organization strategically aligned around suppliers, clients, competitors, the industry—and any potential threats. Because if you are not aware of the forces outside of yourself, your team, and your organization, then you will be shaped by them—frequently, in both unexpected and unpleasant ways.

You make your decisions, and then your decisions make you. When you can see the bigger picture, you'll be making more informed decisions.

There's a complex interplay between what we try to impose on the world from the inside-out and what the world imposes on us from the outside-in.

Understanding this relationship increases the probability that you'll make better decisions that make you... better.

A PATHWAY TO
PERSONAL GROWTH

I NSPIRING OTHERS TO be the best versions of themselves is an integral part of a leader's journey. The pathway starts with a commitment to personal growth.

But sustainable, transformative personal growth requires you to reflect on, and at times challenge, your own beliefs and how they drive your behavior. The first step is understanding the intricate relationship between beliefs, thoughts, and behaviors. Then you'll need to look at the outcomes of your behavior and question how the things that happen reinforce the things you believe.

First, let's define some terms.

Beliefs: The things you believe

These are the underlying theories, values, and assumptions you have about the world, shaped by your inborn preferences and predispositions (nature), the way you were raised (nurture)—or, at times, your own inner running monologue (narrative). Beliefs inform your deepest meaning-making, from religious and political beliefs, to the relatively trivial, like your preferences in beverages and sports teams.

Takeaway: The things you believe inform your way of thinking.

Mindset: Your way of thinking

This determines how you interact with and interpret the world around you. Given the millions of inner beliefs you have and the millions of social environments you operate in, your mindset is as unique as a fingerprint, and the actions that you take are based on what you think is the most effective pathway to success.

Takeaway: Your way of thinking informs the things you do.

Behaviors: The things you do

Behaviors are actions, the things you do to effect change—whether small or large—and impose your will on the world. Without self-awareness, the approach you take will typically follow your unconscious thought patterns. Often that will seem like the only way to go until someone else in the same situation takes a different approach and gets the same, if not better, results.

<u>Takeaway:</u> The things you do affect the things that happen.

Outcomes: The things that happen

Outcomes are results influenced by how you behave. If you are successful, you'll probably continue to think and behave in the same ways. What's the incentive to change, right? Only when things go wrong or derail, will you (maybe) start to question yourself.

<u>Takeaway:</u> The things that happen reinforce the things you believe.

And... now you're back at the beginning!

FROM SELF-AWARENESS TO SELF-MASTERY

Some people operate from a closed-loop feedback system. That means that they embrace outcomes of their behavior that support their beliefs. But if the outcome doesn't match their beliefs, if it challenges their ego, then it must be a fluke, an outlier. For example: "This pitch has always worked before—that group just isn't technical enough to understand."

When you operate from an open-loop feedback system, you are more likely to examine outcomes of your behaviors and measure them against your beliefs. You get curious. Outcomes are not taken simply as a reinforcement of everything you hold to be true—or as an outlier.

With open-loop feedback, you can self-correct your behavior based on the reality of the situation, without your ego throwing up barriers. Now you're approaching self-awareness, the first crucial step on the journey toward self-mastery.

Self-awareness

Self-awareness starts with examining the origins of your nature, nurture, and narrative. How do you approach problems and challenges? And why is that?

Next, understand how your beliefs and behaviors have been formed, reformed, and reinforced throughout your life. A robust psychometric assessment and a good guide—a coach or a therapist, for example—can help. Online surveys and magazine articles, though? Probably not.

Self-management

Once you are aware of your preferences and predispositions, you can begin to consider how they help or hinder your approach to life. For example, you may find that you are overly controlling or overly competitive. This can show up in all sorts of areas, from work projects to a game of tennis with your child.

You may reconfirm the helpfulness of your beliefs… but you may also find that while they were helpful in another time and place, in the early stages of your career, for example, they are not always helpful now. (Or maybe never were!)

When you discover how you get in your own way, you can build "guard rails" around the more extreme excesses of your behaviors. That's self-management.

Self-development

Once you've built those guard rails, you can double down on your natural strengths, highly tuned skills and capabilities, as well as leaning into complementary areas of development— any new, unnatural, or untapped abilities. Now that you've protected the downside, it's time to swing for the fences in a way that can really change the game.

Self-mastery

When you achieve self-mastery, you respond to what the situation demands, according to the circumstances and the team's capabilities, instead of being driven by your natural predispositions, your pride—or your ego. In some cases, you will need to stand up and lead, and in others, you'll need to sit down and follow.

For a leader, self-mastery means knowing when to intervene and when to put the team ahead of the individual. It requires you to flex along the continuum of leadership—from a driving, pacesetting style at one end to a facilitative, empowering style at the other.

To achieve sustainable and transformative personal growth, you'll have to understand and evaluate the underlying values and assumptions you use to inform your decision-making. This helps you become as independent as possible from your biases and blind spots. You'll also need to do the harder work of removing your desires and reducing the impact of your ego—of finding out the truth about who you really are.

The beloved children's television host Fred Rogers said, "Discovering the truth about ourselves is a lifetime's work, but it's worth the effort." The surprising part is that doing this work can have an enormous impact on those around you: When you've become the best version of yourself, you can inspire others to do the same.

THE BACK BURNER

BECAUSE WORKING LIVES are focused on driving results, managing performance, and keeping things on track, we too often try to solve problems with immediate action rather than reflective thought.

You may respond that identifying the challenge, evaluating options, and rapidly implementing the "best" solution works fine for you. In the short term, that may be true. But in the long term, such temporary, transactional resolutions can fail to address underlying issues, and soon, you're revisiting the same problems again and again. It's stressful, unproductive, and exhausting.

The prefrontal cortex is the brain's executive functioning mechanism. It's built to analyze simple, straightforward problems and provide solutions. Processing information at less than 100 bits per second, it tends toward linear thinking and goal-directed behavior—systematic, step-by-step, straight-line thinking and doing. For example, examining data, using logic and rules to problem-solve, or completing tasks; mental functions that operate in response to new and challenging demands.

The subconscious mind, in contrast, is far, far more powerful. It recognizes more complex patterns and forms creative, systemic, and strategic solutions. Processing information at over 10 million bits per second, the subconscious tends toward non-linear thinking, making unexpected connective leaps.

We're all familiar with insightful a-ha moments that happen when we're driving or sitting on a plane, showering or out on a long walk. These revelations represent the subconscious brain—"the Back Burner"—at work. If we intentionally use the Back Burner to problem-solve by creating the conditions under which such insights thrive, then what were once random, infrequent and unpredictable insights will begin to happen more and more often.

In our quick-turnaround, microwaved world, the Back Burner taps the subconscious slow cooker to solve complex, nuanced issues in amazingly innovative, comprehensive ways.

Using this technique can be a significant differentiator and a competitive advantage—a secret weapon. You can pick up on themes in employee feedback, notice patterns your clients don't, and spot industry and marketplace trends faster than competitors.

Here's the Back Burner's four step-process:

STEP 1: Determine a time limit for issue resolution

- Inform key stakeholders about the time frame.

- 72 hours is ideal. With less time, the slow cooker can't do its job. With more you can lose focus.

- Let stakeholders know you'll follow up after you have answers, no sooner. You're creating space for the subconscious to do its work without adding other people's anxieties into the mix.

STEP 2: Review key information

- Clearly identify the issue.

- Gather relevant data. More work for that executive function...

- Resist the temptation to arrive at a premature conclusion. This is time for executive functioning to take a back seat.

STEP 3: Set aside quiet pockets of time

- Within the 72-hour time frame, engage in fine motor activities such as driving, walking, gardening, exercising, or doing a puzzle. These things deliberately divert your brain from thinking about the problem in front of you.

- Limit distractions like television, social media and especially, anything related to the problem, that can command your attention.

- Let the brain drift. What you're looking for are situations in which the linear brain is half-engaged, and the subconscious is free to work.

STEP 4: Capture the a-ha moments

- Be prepared to record thoughts when they materialize.

- Text yourself, record a voice memo, type a phone note, or use good old-fashioned pen and paper.

- Socialize the insights. Talk with people you trust. Evaluate the pros and cons. And confirm that the related actions are robust. Every a-ha needs to be tested for practicality.

The Back Burner gives the subconscious brain space. In our task-oriented, busy lives, this approach helps leaders thoughtfully develop creative, innovative capabilities.

John Steinbeck said problems that seem difficult at night can be resolved by the morning if the "committee of sleep" has worked on them. So let your brain do the heavy lifting through rest. When we're solving problems, silence is where the magic happens. If you trust the process, the answers will come—along with better decisions, greater calm, and sustainable, significant outcomes.

FREEING YOURSELF FROM THE LIMITS OF IDENTITY

S ELF-IMPOSED DEFINITIONS OF identity can be helpful. For example: "I am a command-and-control leader." What you are saying is that when you are in charge, you like to be directive. Here's another example: "I am a people-person." Clearly, you prefer people to tasks, profits, etc.

When you define yourself these ways, the underlying implication is that your natural strengths don't require any mitigating or finetuning, which is a fair trade-off for any potential downsides to your approach. In fact, doing the opposite of what's natural for you—being a facilitative leader or being solitary and shy—would be unnatural.

Being a "command-and-control leader" is certainly useful in situations that require clear and explicit direction— during a crisis, for instance. But making and reinforcing statements about your identity makes you more attached to your identity, which creates a rigidity that can hinder you. Your directive, controlling approach will yield very different results when you are *not* in a crisis.

In other words, if you see your natural self as one way and never another, only *this* and not *that*, you can develop blind spots—a resistance to operating in "the other" mode, whatever that is.

The more you reinforce your self-imposed definitions of identity, the more likely they are to become boundaries. Your focus narrows. You stay in a very thin lane of your own making.

Worse, sometimes self-definitions start off with a slightly negative spin.

- "I am not very technical."

- "I am no subject-matter expert."

- "I am not great with numbers."

- "I am not a good project manager."

- "I am not a natural leader."

Over time, your fixed identity—the way you see yourself, either positively or negatively—can become a barrier to your success. That very thin lane of your own making can start to feel constrained, imposed—and unchangeable. You'll eventually get stuck there.

PRACTICING VERSATILITY

Versatility is the key to getting unstuck. When you are versatile, you are flexible. You adapt. When you broaden your self-definition to incorporate such versatility, you can pivot—not just personally, but within your team and organization, too.

Eventually, you may see your own preferences and predispositions not as ways to define your identity, but as the first set of tools you were given. Developing "the other" mode, whatever that is for you, means gathering more tools, becoming more versatile, and that means growth. Your previous, rather limiting thoughts could transform into possibility-filled ideas like these:

- "I don't naturally think technically, but I'm exploring that style more often now."

- "I am excited to build that subject-matter expertise."

- "I've worked with numbers before—I mean, we all have a little bit, right?—and I'll lean on others when I need help."

- "I'll make the effort to figure out how to be a more capable project manager."

- "I am willing to lead and I'm ready to learn how."

There are times when you must push beyond comfortable boundaries and show faith in your talents by trying out new things. And as you adapt to new conditions, you may realize that many of your beliefs about your identity are self-limiting; that some of those boundaries are, in fact, self-imposed.

You may even decide to abandon what is no longer serving you.

The difference between having a fixed identity—with no emphasis on growth, learning, and change—versus being open to developing all aspects of yourself: that is the difference between being a decent manager and a great leader. Why not give yourself the freedom of versatility? Lean into learning and leave those fixed "I am"s behind.

HINDSIGHT, INSIGHT, FORESIGHT

REFLECTING ON THE past—*hindsight*—can develop your *insight* about present situations. In turn that insight, that awareness, is critical in figuring out the future—it's called *foresight*. Being intentional about these three sense-making activities—hindsight, insight, and foresight—can help you predict patterns and outcomes more accurately.

HINDSIGHT

"Hindsight is 20/20" means it's obvious after it's happened.

Hindsight itself presents a great opportunity too many people miss. Because in the heat of the battle it's hard to think clearly. (That's why the coaches stay on the sidelines, that's why the generals sit on the hill.) When you're consumed by the details of a rapidly changing environment, you're less likely to spot pivotal pathways or valuable connections, and because you're in an emotionally heightened state, you may misread the hidden forces at work. Plus, if you've narrowed your focus on taking care of what's right in front of you, you can miss both critical information and the bigger patterns at play.

But the opportunity people miss about hindsight is that if you're intentional about it, it's as if you're watching the tapes, like football coaches do obsessively after every game, analyzing them in a way you never could in real time. Generals do something similar in an after-action review.

On the other side of a supposed win or a supposed loss, everything is far clearer. You can see, feel, and think about all the information—especially the stuff that may not have been obviously relevant at the time. You can more easily identify hidden forces at play and understand how your efforts, or lack thereof, have contributed to the results.

You shouldn't just analyze your losses. Coaches don't. Generals don't. They analyze every process and every play in every game and every event—including the big wins— to see how they won and how they could do even better next time.

INSIGHT

Doing a deep dive into the past gives you insight into current situations. You may come to acknowledge, for example, that a supposedly "great success" wasn't all that great in the end because it led to unintended, undesirable consequences. For example, your team won a huge contract the business couldn't handle, which created difficulties across the organization and with other clients.

Conversely, you may come to appreciate that an incident everyone considered a "great failure" actually produced some unintended benefits. For example, your team's production line shut down but after you got it running, you'd learned how to prevent a shutdown from happening again; your team grew closer through the shared experience; they demonstrated commitment, perseverance, and the capability to deal with crisis; and weathering the crisis boosted the team's confidence.

When you are an insightful leader, you approach inquiry with curiosity and spirit—and your optimism can be infectious. Ideally, your team will cultivate the same good habits: Figuring out what went well and what went badly, applying that knowledge to future experiences, developing situational flexibility and resilience—it's all part of a learning orientation that will hopefully rub off on the larger organization, too.

FORESIGHT

Yesterday's hindsight and today's insight give you foresight—the capacity to calculate what might happen tomorrow. No one can control the future, but the more you anticipate and plan for tomorrow, the more you increase the probability of positive and desirable outcomes for you and your team.

On an individual level, understanding how you navigated a previous challenge can help you identify your strengths and weaknesses while you prepare for the next one. Feeling confident about your team and your ability to lead them and feeling confident about their own ability to lay the groundwork for upcoming events, increases the likelihood of success.

Philosopher Søren Kierkegaard asserted that life can only be understood backwards, but it must be lived forwards. He's spot on. To learn anything significant, to expand your perspective—to grow—you must begin by reflecting on the past: the good, the bad, and the ugly.

When you leverage the information you've gained from yesterday's experiences, you'll better understand today. And with a head full of knowledge and a soul full of wisdom, you can lead your team confidently through the uncertainties of tomorrow.

A FRAMEWORK FOR DECISION-MAKING

DECISION-MAKING. IT'S ONE of the hardest parts of leadership. Even the clearest-thinking, most capable and confident leaders sometimes worry over the unintended impacts of their choices. And rightly so.

The higher the level of leadership you're operating at, the more complex the scenarios. A successful outcome usually needs numerous inputs and efforts from multiple people. That means any significant decision requires a leader to sort through masses of conflicting information—and that can strain anyone's cognitive processing.

Plus, the closer you are to the top, the more significant, far-reaching, substantive, and long-lasting the impact of your decisions become. A good decision can accelerate your career; a bad one can tank it. And of course, your decisions impact your business, too, for good or ill—as well as your employees and clients and even their families.

So when a tough decision wakes you up at 3am and won't leave you alone, how do you avoid second-guessing, eliminate unproductive thoughts and ultimately get yourself back to sleeping through the night? Following a decision-making methodology can help.

Imagine a scenario where you are figuring out whether to let go of a well-loved and long-serving employee whose work quality and attitude have recently, but consistently, dipped. Now walk through the following three steps, asking yourself these kinds of questions:

Step #1: Get the right information

Gather evidence

Questions: Is the evidence second-hand, or have I seen proof myself? When did the employee's performance and attitude drop off? Are there objective methods of measuring these things? Do I have enough relevant, factual evidence?

Examine assumptions

Questions: Does the organization have an archetype of what a "typical" employee looks like? Does the culture value being "well-loved and long-serving?" How does the organization deal with attitude and work performance issues in other parts of the business? In other words, can I clearly see how my own and others' assumptions about the situation inform the course of action?

Understand the context

Questions: What does the team look like, and what are they saying about the situation? Does the employee bring value outside of their performance? Which controllable environmental factors—such as more training or team structure—may be contributing to the employee's attitude? In other words, have I considered every angle?

Determine if there are better options

Questions: Have I thought through alternative scenarios? Is this a "one-and-done" decision—the person stays or the person goes—or are there secondary decisions to be made that can result in off-ramps? For example, to get back on track, the employee might benefit from a reduced job scope, a reassignment of duties, a departmental transfer, or unpaid leave.

Step #2: Consider the timeframe for decision-making

Figure out the urgency

Questions: Is there a timeframe around the decision? Do I need to decide now? What are the consequences of inaction—intentional or otherwise?

Identify if you're on track

Questions: Once the decision is made, what will indicate that things are happening according to plan? For instance, if you gave the employee a 60-day improvement plan, how would you gauge if behavior and attitude are getting better? And, if there's no change, when and how will you intervene?

Define what "success" means

Questions: Do you have a clear outline of what a successful, or at least reasonable, outcome looks like? How else will you bring closure to the process?

Step #3: Evaluate the landscape of possibility

In many cases, the most likely outcome is a complex one, with both good and bad elements. For example, removing that difficult and underperforming employee (good), may come at the cost of losing their years of experience, which you'll have to pay more for—literally or figuratively—to bring back in (bad). And, although the employee's removal may lift team morale (good), their absence may disrupt other business functions (bad).

Imagine the worst-case scenario

Questions: What is the most negative consequence of your decision and what is the probability of it happening? How can you mitigate organizational risk?

Imagine the best-case scenario

Questions: What is the most positive consequence of your decision and what is the probability of it happening?

Consider the potential of a hybrid or neutral case

Questions: Can your decision result in a "mixed bag" of consequences? And what is the probability of that happening?

Making decisions can be difficult, especially when you're leading at the highest organizational levels. Following a decision-making methodology gives you the structure to work through complex details faster and more productively. You'll be calmer, too, meaning you'll be sleeping more soundly through the night and seeing a lot less of "3am."

EXPAND OR CONTRACT, IT'S UP TO YOU

TIMES OF GREAT chaos and change can shake you up. And after you catch your breath, you may retreat from the world—and contract. But there's an alternative: You can choose to take a deep breath, push through the initial shock and discomfort—and expand. Your perspective might expand, too. If it does, maybe you'll be able to see times of great chaos and change instead, as times of great reinvention, reimagining, and repositioning.

The expand and contract of breath is automatic. Rarely, if ever, do you think about the 20,000 times each day that you move air through your lungs, instinctively inhaling to expand and exhaling to contract. Expanding or contracting in your professional life is more deliberate.

The first day in a role, meeting an important client, publicly managing a crisis, trying out a new skill—this is what contracting can look like at work. Your body is feeling tense, your mind anxious. On high alert, you're probably holding back from action and engagement because your attention is focused inward, on your own needs.

In contrast, when circumstances are familiar, stable, and favorable, you're more likely to exude confidence. You're trusting yourself, looking outward to the future with hope, and engaging others—this is what expanding can look like at work.

Contracting can certainly benefit you in times of extreme stress, such as a life-or-death threat against your survival, but it will never let you thrive. That's what expansion is for—and it can benefit you individually, collectively within your team, and organizationally.

INDIVIDUALLY

Leadership requires—even demands—that you expand. Part of your role is to set a course based on today's knowns while simultaneously figuring out how to adapt and evolve to unknown circumstances. Expansion can be uncomfortable, of course it can! There's no map and no compass.

But if you can survive what may often feel like stormy waters, you'll benefit. Here's the biggest upside: You'll shape the future instead of being shaped by it, and you'll disrupt the world instead of being disrupted by it.

COLLECTIVELY

Expanding collectively occurs when you've set up the team for success, despite the chaos and change happening around them. Encouraging open viewpoints and wide perspectives among team members can help the group discover unique connections and patterns they wouldn't otherwise see.

Learning new skills, training, finding creative approaches to do more with less, and leaning on each other, are other ways the team can grow through tough times together—and benefit.

ORGANIZATIONALLY

Most organizations contract in difficult times. Cost-cutting, downsizing, reigning in expenses, and shelving new projects are examples. But a well-prepared organization that has retained resources during the good times has the advantage of being able to invest—and thus, expand—in uncertain times. A downturn can also be used by the company to experiment or put pressure on competitors who have been complacent during the good times; competitors who haven't prepared quite as strategically.

Even if your organization hasn't prepared for challenging times, you can still benefit from an expansive mindset by thinking about questions like these:

- How can you capture market share from troubled competitors?

- How can you build deeper relationships with your clients, especially those who are struggling?

- How can you come out on the other side of the storm with your boats intact and the wind in your sails?

EXPAND OR CONTRACT, IT'S UP TO YOU

In some cases, you may need to contain resources in one area to deploy in another. Investing in R&D at the expense of advertising, for instance. Or contract in the short term to prepare for expansion. For example, outsourcing non-critical activities like administration while the company gets ready to internally deliver the largest deal in its history. Great leaders make these decisions intentionally. Remember that you are not just in control, you are in charge.

When the stakes are higher, the impact of your decisions is bigger. Don't forget that times of great chaos and change have the potential to become times of great reinvention, reimagining, and repositioning. And the possibilities can be exciting.

As a leader, you get to shape the future you want to live in, and you get to inspire others to do it with you. So the next time you feel yourself contracting—stepping back, narrowing your attention, and focusing on your own needs—you can decide to inhale deeply and expand—stepping in, broadening your attention, and focusing on others and the organization.

A better future is waiting for you, your team, and the organization. Here's the good news: All of it is up to you.

THE STORIES
YOU TELL

STORIES PROVIDE COMFORT in challenging times. They create connection and develop identity. Stories spark imagination and inspire us to face collective challenges. They give us a sense of meaning, help us envision a better future. There is great power in weaving together purposeful elements into the stories you tell about yourself, others, the organization, and the future. That's why history's greatest leaders have also been great storytellers.

THE STORIES YOU TELL YOURSELF

The stories you tell about yourself come in two varieties: conscious (the ones you're aware of) and subconscious (the ones you're not).

Conscious stories are grounded in your background and upbringing, your values and predispositions, your moments of triumph and failure. But whatever stories you consciously tell yourself and others, there's another voice inside you as well, one that arises out of your memories, instincts, thoughts, feelings, and experiences. It writes your subconscious stories. Like a 24-hour news radio, it's always on, replaying your weaknesses or reminding you of your strengths. It can be gentle, but it's more often quick to judge—and it doesn't forget.

Part of becoming a great leader is learning how to mitigate and manage your conscious and subconscious voices (if you don't control them and their stories, they will control you) to craft a compelling outer narrative that you can bring to life for others. Those others might include your team, your organization, your clients, the industry, and the media. Telling your compelling narrative will allow you to build connections, demonstrate credibility, and reinforce a particular company image, motto, or approach.

The stories you tell about yourself might include an inspirational origin story about overcoming hardship. Or maybe you incorporate later-in-life experiences that humbly highlight your weaknesses, demonstrate your grit when faced with adversity, or showcase your values.

While embellishment is only natural, authenticity should be at the core, because if you're open about your experiences, principles, and desires, you'll make deeper, more genuine connections. And when you reinforce common values—such as humility, hard work, compassion, competence, credibility, fun, or perseverance—your audience will develop a shared sense of meaning, which can lead to greater cohesiveness.

THE STORIES YOU TELL ABOUT OTHERS

Leaders connect people and reinforce camaraderie by telling stories about the ways they're bound together. For example, difficult experiences, mutual fears, shared dreams, a similar perspective, collective history, values, or even a common enemy.

Shared expressions can be part of the team's story, too, and they might sound like this:

- "Remember the Anderson project? Good people like us prevail in the end!"

- "We are not the kind of team to take this lying down! Unless we're catching some rays at the annual beach party."

- "We've got each other's backs—especially when we're wrecking accounting in laser tag!"

Whether it's a motto, a mission, or a saying, one thing's for sure—everyone knows every word.

THE STORIES YOU TELL ABOUT THE ORGANIZATION

The leader shapes the organization's identity by creating narratives around key successes or failures, historical milestones, industry position and/or a unique set of competencies. When they're told and told again, these stories can become an integral part of the culture. And as they are passed from generation to generation, this company folklore strengthens individual connections, collective identity, and group cohesion.

Stories you tell about the organization help anchor each team member's daily actions to its wider goals. By drawing out a shared sense of meaning, you create deeper connections that can lead to better communication and collaboration.

THE STORIES YOU TELL ABOUT THE FUTURE

A leader's vision of the future should be grounded in reality, with an aspirational stretch toward possibility. That's how inspiration works.

Good stories remind us of what we've achieved in the past, as well as the capabilities and character that got us there—the capabilities and character that define our culture. This gives us faith that down the road, we can handle any challenge that comes our way if we work together and maybe even paint a picture of what our dreams look like.

So… what stories will you tell?

THE LIMITS OF
LINEAR THINKING

L INEAR THINKING IS a reactive, give-and-take, straight-
line approach. You respond to whatever happens as if
you're playing a simple game of checkers. Checkers has basic,
identical pieces in two colors that can mostly only move one
square at a time. At best maybe you get lucky and can make
an occasional double-jump, but usually it's back and forth.

At the most basic level, linear thinking can look like this: If
I'm cold, I put on a jacket. If I'm hungry, I eat. If something
is broken, I fix it. If someone shakes my hand, I shake their
hand back. Your automatic—primal—responses, can lead
to short-term wins. I'm warm, my appetite is satisfied, the
thing is fixed, I've made a connection.

When you're operating at a higher level of leadership,
though, you're functioning in a more complex way, and
you're considering different variables. You're strategically

responding to what happens, thinking several steps ahead about the movements you'll make. This kind of complex thinking is more like playing chess.

Chess has six types of pieces, each with their own special look and rules about where and how they can move. And knocking your opponent's pieces off the board is not enough; you have a long-term goal of capturing their king. In chess, short-term thinking won't cut it. Game play is longer, more theoretical, more intentional.

In business, as in chess, linear thinking is limiting. Here are a few areas where a more complex, chess-like approach can lead to a winning mentality in the long term.

DECISION-MAKING

Your role as a leader is to use your cognitive, social, and emotional intelligence to make sense of the world. When you are interpreting information about a situation, you are using cognitive intelligence. Having social intelligence means being aware of your actions within a social setting. Your team members' actions, too. Knowing and taking into consideration your own and others' emotions contributes to your emotional intelligence.

In this three-dimensional approach to decision-making, understanding the relationships between the different cognitive, social, and emotional variables at play—people, team dynamics, competition, experience, scale of impact, and organizational politics, for instance—is critical. Condensing, streamlining, and codifying the information you've gathered helps you make the most informed decision. You've simplified things for others so they can take the next step, though you've already thought two or three steps beyond that.

GROWTH

Linear thinking is incremental, for example creating a budget with a single digit increase on the prior year. Quantum thinking is exponential, and it's required to make things faster, better, more responsive, more accessible— by multiples. Growth by multiples is vastly different from percentage growth. Increasing growth by 10x, a quantum-thinking approach to growth, requires completely different thinking than increasing revenues by 10%.

Preparing for exponential growth—like chess—requires every move you make today to be aimed at the future. This means looking up, over, and around the situation instead of staring straight at it.

PROBLEM-SOLVING

A simple question from a member of your team can have hidden depths. And because you have more information, more history, and a broader perspective than most of your team, your answers can carry more weight than you think—they can even be transformative.

For example, a team member comes into your office saying, "Our competition has just launched a new product and we didn't see it coming! What do I do?"

If you're playing chess, your answer can shape the organization's culture, define its values, and set the tone for action. It can also demonstrate what is important to you as the leader, as well as the company. It can connect people (or not!) to a shared perspective or a common story. So be explicit about expectations and priorities.

SUCCESS

Anyone who has been through a well-run change project can recognize that success is not linear—there's no such thing as a straight line from the "past state" to your desired "future state." Although it may look like that from the outside, success is made up of daily battles (lost and won), a constant push toward your goals, and a realistic perspective that you can't win 'em all, every day.

Progress depends on building a solid base of people and processes, being clear about measures of success, and finding meaningful ways to celebrate the milestone wins along the way. Consider the trajectory, not just today's data, when setting objectives. And amid the daily battles, keep your chess head on: Think strategically and don't become reactive.

RELATIONSHIPS

Allowing yourself to be reactive and get emotionally highjacked can limit your ability to read the room clearly and consistently. It can stop you from building deeper relationships based on trust. So as a general rule, don't ascribe to malice what can be explained by incompetence, ignorance, complacency, or lack of interest.

For example, if someone ignores you or doesn't prioritize your request and you don't know why, you might fill that vacuum of information with negative thinking: They don't care about you, they are deliberately undermining you, they are only interested in themselves. Usually, they just have other things to do—you're just not in their sightline.

Two solid strategies: Respond, don't react. And as a first pass, assume neutral intent.

Because you are the leader, you should aspire to be more like a chess player than a checkers champ. Your game is a long one, with infinite possibilities, and lots of moving pieces, and so it requires a highly strategic approach. Removing the limitations of a linear approach can allow you to win—and maybe even master the board.

MASTERING
THE INVISIBLE

WHAT HAPPENS WHEN the factors that drive results—
such as good momentum, effective teamwork,
trusted relationships, market dynamics, client relationships,
and an inclusive culture—can't readily be controlled? When
you're trying to create change, how can you get comfortable
with intangibles like "brand" or a professional network that
can't be touched or measured?

When you master the invisible, you're able to see, consider, and
harness the unobservable, the unseen, and the uncontrollable.
This skill is central to the sense-making role of a leader,
because at higher executive levels—CEO, for example—you
cannot sustain success just by solving pressing, one-off issues.
You need to be proficient at designing sustainable solutions.
Systems thinking—seeing the big picture, looking at wholes
versus parts, examining relationships—can help.

To minimize risk, reduce variability, and increase transparency—in other words, to take charge of the unobservable, the unseen, and the uncontrollable—it's important to build a system that recognizes your own underlying personal motivators, hidden team dynamics, and unseen forces in the world.

YOUR OWN UNDERLYING PERSONAL MOTIVATORS

- Personal motivators can be things like financial success, recognition, fun, power, security, quality of life, family, and relationships.

- If you have little self-awareness, meaning you don't really understand who you are and what motivates you, you'll be unconsciously steered by these personal motivators. You'll struggle to figure out how they impact your thoughts and behavior.

- But when you better understand what drives you, you'll have more awareness and control. You can say "no" more clearly, confidently, and firmly. Then you can steer yourself in the direction you want.

- Learning who you are and what you do well—and not so well—impacts your team, too. Understanding what you can do less of (actions that hinder others) and what you can do more of (actions that accelerate others' success) will tell you when to stand up and lead and when to sit down and follow. You'll reduce your ego's influence and be further along the pathway to self-mastery.

HIDDEN TEAM DYNAMICS

- Whether they are aware of it or not, team members, too, bring their unique personal motivators to the group.

- If you as the leader don't see and harness each team member's motivation, the team's rewards can be misaligned—and you'll all be focusing on the wrong things. Does the group want a bonus or a week off? A week off or company recognition?

- You must ask about what they want, listen to the answers, and effectively communicate the desired rewards for achieving success.

- If you're not rewarding team members individually, finding a solution that works for everyone can be a problem. Not every team member has the same motivations, and if they do miraculously line up, it might not happen at the same time. For example, a person who usually prefers time off might need a bonus this time and someone who usually likes praise may want a few vacation days.

- Managing relationship dynamics is also important. Depending on the size of the team, you could be dealing with a lot of perspectives and judgments! It's tricky to figure out who team members see as lazy or as a hard worker, as bossy or as a pushover. And some people might feel certain members are getting preferential treatment while others are getting passed over, for example. Paying attention to verbal and non-verbal communication is key.

- Organizational dynamics like culture, structure, and situational specifics come into play, too, and if you don't accurately take those factors into consideration, you'll run the risk of disconnection by enabling behavior by the team that is not aligned with the context (i.e., geography, industry, time of year, buying/selling cycle), or the strategic direction of the organization.

UNSEEN FORCES IN THE WORLD

- It's the leader's job to simplify and make sense of the unseen—and often complex—forces in the world.

- An example of an unseen force is when a competitor unexpectedly launches a new product.

- Your response to this may be determined by, among other things, your perception of the market, how you generally react to surprises, the quality of the launched product, the company's marketplace position, a client's receptiveness to new ideas, or the depth of your relationship with them.

- You can respond in different ways. Telling your team,

"Don't worry, there's nothing in this!" is one option. Or maybe you move quickly and decisively into action mode, reaching out to your biggest clients to gauge reactions. Alternatively, you may prepare internally by launching a market research initiative to test if the product will stick. You might simply watch the situation play out. Whatever choice you make, confidence and intentionality are key.

MASTERING THE INVISIBLE

A reduction in spending. A curb on travel expenses. A ban on overtime. These actions produce temporary, transactional results. But direct, hands-on management of numbers, people, and processes will only get you so far. When you shift your perspective, you stop believing that you can press a button, charge up a certain team member, or in any other way apply direct brute force to a single variable to yield a better outcome.

You don't have to be a wizard or a jedi to master invisibles like "brand" or a professional network, but you will have to take a much broader and higher perspective. In other words, start operating at a systems level by addressing the broader variables that influence the system as a whole. It's a less obvious and less tactical approach but it will yield long-term, highly impactful results.

Mastering the invisible demands emotional maturity, intelligence, awareness of social systems, and conceptual fluency—tools that help you observe, think about, and manage your motivations, team dynamics, and the unseen forces in the world. Over time and with practice, you'll be more in control of the uncontrollable.

THE LEADER AS A FUTURE SHAPER

THIS SECTION CONSIDERS the mission dimension of leadership.

As we touched on in the opening section, a leader orients toward the future. A leader is a *future shaper*. Future shapers have a clear <u>vision</u> and an energetic, systemic <u>bias for action</u>. The results they create for their teams are successful, sustainable, and strategic—in a word, transformative. And they do it by embracing and managing an uncertain future.

KEY COMPETENCIES

Vision

Imagining a way of being in the world that doesn't currently exist.

A bias for action

In order to shape the future, leaders are compelled to find actions that bring the vision to life. They see the potential for action everywhere.

IN SHORT

People turn to leaders to build a better tomorrow, to help them leave a mark by having a dream and bringing it to life. Great leaders are purposeful and strategic, and they use a compelling vision to lead change, which gives people a deeper *sense of purpose*.

As you read through the next ten chapters, think about how you show up as a Future Shaper. Have you created and communicated a compelling vision? How have you brought it to life?

TIME, TRUTH, AND TRUST

LEADERS LOOKING TO shape the future must be strategic. Strategy requires *time* to develop, and it also depends on *truth*—seeing the world as it is. And to bring strategy to life, you'll need *trust* between you and the team, as well as within it.

Time, truth, and trust are critical and connected but often rare aspects of the working environment, particularly at the top. Shortages of any of those three can have negative personal and professional consequences. Poor self-management (through a lack of time), insufficient clarity (through a lack of truth), and a culture of fear (through a lack of trust)—these can make strategic planning and implementing a coherent strategy nearly impossible.

TIME

"I don't control my schedule; my schedule controls me." How many times have you thought this? Said this? Most leaders rarely take time off. Even if you are physically removed from your working environment, genuine disconnection can be frowned upon, and in some circles, considered career suicide.

The impacts of globalization, technology, complexity, and marketplace competition, plus the expectations of short-term success, all limit the time you'd ideally spend strategically reflecting, gathering information, evaluating options, and planning. If you feel time crunched, it will eventually take a toll on your leadership effectiveness. You'll rush decision-making. You'll execute poorly.

Here are a few high-level ways you can be more in control of your time:

- Leverage the visible infrastructures—for example, closing the office door to focus on important, reflective tasks—and the invisible infrastructures—reducing the frequency of your meetings or the number of attendees. Doing this protects your time boundaries and ensures that you are efficient with tasks and connected to people in intentional ways.

- Free up mental energy for your most essential tasks. Deprioritize, delegate, or defer action items. Taking them off your plate gives you more time to focus on critical tasks.

- As the leader, you are comparable to the car's engine, and your team's capabilities are like a car's gears. Gears convert the leader's energy into motion and determine how effectively leadership is translated into action/accomplishment. A team with the right gears leverages the leader's energy, allowing you to move more quickly, and with less effort. So, leveraging your team both helps you conserve your energy and use your time effectively.

If you are not in control of your time, your stress will cause you to have a distorted view of the truth.

TRUTH

It has been said that the first casualty of war is the truth. To draw a parallel to business, in most organizations, the first casualty of a promotion is the truth. What that means is that by the time information reaches senior leaders, it's often diluted or filtered, and the facts adjusted or blurred.

Many of history's worst business failures resulted from an absence of "speaking truth to power"—most notably from lower-level executives whose communication to people in authority positions lacked transparency. If the truth is compromised, even the most skilled leaders can experience a disorienting sense of wariness, skepticism, and paranoia about what's real and what's not.

Here are a few high-level ways you can improve the quality of information that you receive:

- Consider how you are asking questions. It is your job as a leader to identify errors and determine an issue's root cause. However, if your questions are only ever accusatory and lead to "flaming" others, then your team is likely to clam up. Or they may present a version of events that purposely leaves out important details. How you ask questions and how you respond to answers can lead to more accurate information.

- Consider who you are asking questions of. It's often said that there are three sides to every story—yours, mine, and what actually happened. Triangulate information from trusted sources, then find ways to add four, five, or six sides. This will help you sort through the noise, including well-meaning but misguided feedback. And you'll see more clearly in those situations where others are only seeing what they want to see.

- Seek truth in unexpected places. For the sake of efficiency, a leader will go to the alleged source of information. But if you also gather information from peripheral people—people apart from the project manager or the most senior person present when an issue occurs—you will get another perspective without compromising confidentiality or reporting lines.

- Engage consiglieres, mentors, or trusted advisors inside and outside the organization. These relationships help you identify systemic issues, as well as patterns that pop up in other functions, departments, companies, or industries. You'll be able to contextualize information, and as a result, your actions will be more constructive and sustainable.

If you do not improve the quality of information that you receive, you will have a distorted view of the truth, which will lead to your lack of trust.

TRUST

Offices can be ridden with internal politics. Ambitions, styles, goals, and personalities might clash—especially if colleagues outwardly agree with the team goals when in fact their inward motivations and ambitions don't align.

In these make-or-break environments, where one bad decision or one poorly executed plan can tank a career, trusting others can feel unnatural. Trust means being vulnerable, giving your colleagues—who are also "rivals" in contention for accolades, resources, credit, or promotions—information that can be used as ammunition. To stay safe, people keep their walls up, and information gets withheld or spun.

Here are a few high-level ways you can improve trust levels:

- Management consultants have identified four variables that can contribute to improved trust between colleagues:

job competency, reliability, security (confidence that information won't be used against you), and self-orientation (how much you're focused on yourself compared to how much you're focused on others). Develop environments within your team and the wider organization where trust is earned.

- Encourage open communication. Sometimes saying what needs to be said is tough to pull off, but open dialog among team members can lead to better outcomes if it's done constructively. Pay special attention to situations when communication dries up. Instead of rushing through uncomfortable moments, pause and double-click (or dig deeper)—that's where the juice is.

- Practice "eyes on, hands-off" management—give your team responsibility and autonomy within firm guidelines. And give them the opportunity to earn the right to be left alone.

- Tolerate small mistakes. Consider them part of you and your team's learning process. International bridge captain Alfred Sheinwold said, "Learn all you can from the mistakes of others. You won't have time to make them all yourself." He was onto something.

If you don't trust others, you waste time figuring out who you can trust. And sometimes, you think it's less complicated just to do the work yourself. So you're not adding value to the team, you're compensating for the gaps that you're ultimately responsible for.

You can't have an effective strategy without the time to develop it, the truth of the facts on the ground, and earned trust in the people around you. But with these precious commodities in the bank, you can shape an intentional, authentic, and sound future.

A COMPELLING
VISION

HOW MANY CORPORATE vision statements have you read that sound like they came out of an online "Corporate Vision Generator?" Run-of-the-mill declarations such as "undisputed marketplace leadership," and generic goals like "providing the highest level of service, the broadest selection of products, and the most competitive prices," or "access to diverse services to stay relevant in tomorrow's world"—not very exciting, right?

Vision statements are essential: They communicate the leader's goals to the world and motivate employees to discover personal reasons to meet them. But here's the rub: Creating a unique and meaningful organizational vision requires time—more time than most leaders are willing to give.

So how do you use your time wisely to craft an inspirational statement that captures the story of where the company is today and where it's going? You start with specifics.

DEFINE THE STORY

A vision takes many variables into account. That might include the current state of the organization, the competitive landscape, the existing supply chain, prevalent industry standards, and the organization's present depth and caliber of internal talent.

More importantly, though, a compelling vision details how *your* organization—and not just any organization—can "win" in the future. Again, the details are key. To get your juices flowing, try answering these questions as specifically as possible:

- Where is your organization headed in the next few years?

- What will your organization do to get there? (In other words, how will your company play the game?)

- In academic and business strategist Michael Porter's wise words, "The essence of strategy is choosing what not to do." So where won't the organization go and what aren't you prepared to do?

Are your answers meaninglessly vague and undefined phrases like "undisputed marketplace leadership," or "the most competitive prices" that could apply to almost any company? And if so, what does that say about your organization?

If your answers were generic, revisit those questions and drill down until your answers specifically, uniquely—authentically—describe your organization.

The next step is bringing your vision to life through deeds and words—that's called having a bias for action.

BRING THE STORY TO LIFE THROUGH DEEDS

Deeds help to ensure that your organization's operations are continuously aligned with its vision. Deeds are actions; they are how the organization will get where it wants to go. Here are a few examples.

- Develop a clear business plan. How can you best position your organization to delight your clients? To serve the market? To win in the industry? What actions do you need to take? How can you act in ways that are differentiated, better, and hard to copy? Is the plan tied to the vision?

- Examine internal talents and capabilities. Does the organization have enough skilled, motivated, talented, and capable employees to execute the vision? Will you need to hire additional people?

- Establish scalable infrastructure. Systems and processes should be able to expand, contract, and adapt to meet market demands—can yours do this effectively enough to execute the vision?

- Look closely at partnerships, clients, suppliers, and providers. Do you have the right supply chain and delivery infrastructure to execute the vision?

It's equally important to ask if you are well positioned to execute on the vision beyond a few years. If not, what will you do to bridge the gap?

To recap, these actions will build that bridge: revisiting the business plan, reexamining internal talents and capabilities, reestablishing scalable infrastructure, and looking more closely at partnerships, clients, suppliers, and providers. These will also help you refocus and course correct, if needed.

BRING THE STORY TO LIFE THROUGH WORDS

Businessman Jeff Weiner believes repetition is imperative to making corporate messages stick. His advice: "If you want to get your point across, especially to a broader audience, you need to repeat yourself so often you get sick of hearing yourself say it. And only then will people begin to internalize what you're saying."

So spread the vision. Company-wide town halls, update videos, individual and team meetings, company retreats, and corporate newsletters are ways to say the same words, to tell (and retell) the same story. Different initiatives require different communication skills (large group, on-camera, one-on-one, small group, verbal, written) and you, as the leader, need to be competent at all of them. Or else have a great team behind you that can help you shine! Preferably both.

Brought to life through a leader's deeds and words, a vision is a map and compass. With a compelling vision, you can chart your organization's pathway to success and bridge the gap from today to a better future. Because as the proverb goes, "Where there is no vision, the people perish."

CRAFTING A FLEXIBLE PLAN

S TRATEGIC PLANNING IS breaking down your vision into manageable milestones; it's bridging the gap between strategy and tactics. And while it's not the sexiest skill, it is critical for shaping the future.

Planning preferences exist on a spectrum. At one end, there are individuals who like structure. And if they like structure, they probably like order and control, too. They want to be sure processes are followed, that rules are enforced, that roles and responsibilities are respected, and ultimately, that their plan is adhered to.

On the other end, there are people who value flexibility, adaptability, and spontaneity. They want to be sure there is room to interpret processes, that rules are not binding, that roles and responsibilities are fluid, and ultimately, that their plan is referenced but not definitive.

Although you will gravitate toward either structure or flexibility, it's important to accept—and appreciate—that both approaches have value. Understanding where team members' preferences lie is helpful when planning, too. It gives you the big picture, so that, depending on the situation, everyone can adapt.

MASTERY IS CREATIVITY WITHIN A SYSTEM

Adaptation is an art and a science that requires outsized effort and a clear head. A take on this concept often attributed to Picasso: "Learn the rules like a pro, so you can break them like an artist."

Believe it or not, you can apply this Spanish artist and provocateur's wisdom to something as un-sexy as strategic planning.

Leaders depend on systems to bring vision to life, but if this is all you have, there's no room for innovation. On the other hand, if all you have is creativity, you'll end up with chaos—brilliant content that lacks structure. Think of it like writing music without timing, poetry without meter, architecture without engineering, or art without form.

No plan—no matter how well planned—fully survives contact with reality because life is in charge, not you. True craft in strategic planning is being creative while using, and sometimes stretching, the underlying structures.

In other words, you clearly determine where you're going, but you're less rigid about how you'll get there. That way, you'll have options if there's a hitch with any of the plan's internal assumptions, like organizational capabilities, cost conditions, or competitive positioning. And you'll be able to pivot—which hopefully, should feel more like course corrections than hard lefts—when external variables like interest rates, client requirements, or supply chain structures change.

Just like the world's gifted musicians, poets, architects, and artists, you can use an interplay between structure and flexibility to elevate the mundane and create something more durable, powerful, inspiring, and essential—a bridge to a better future.

THE UPSIDE
OF DOWN

I T'S EASY TO navigate the good times when the market is expanding and everyone's making money. But how do you show up when times get tough, when markets contract, or you're seeing other grim financial indicators like loss of revenue, layoffs, or reductions in services?

You could always panic. But great leaders—strong leaders—look for the upside during the down times. They realize that tough stretches are great opportunities to make smart, strategic decisions around teams, clients, vendors, and competitors, in order to build a more sustainable organization.

YOUR TEAM

During uncertain times, people seek out assurance, security, direction, and community. Maybe even a little inspiration. The biggest upside of down is that you and your team can build organizational capabilities like resilience, shared experiences, and growth opportunities. Just remember that as their leader, you'll need to develop these things for yourself initially—in other words, putting on your own oxygen mask first.

- Develop resilience. When faced with incredibly challenging circumstances, there is an equally incredible chance to develop a courageous mindset.

- Reinforce shared experiences. An obstacle or negative situation can reaffirm connections, commitments, and values plus it may remind team members why they got into the job/company/industry in the first place.

- Provide growth opportunities. As the team collectively builds new skills and experiences—applying lean principles and crisis management are examples—that can serve them in the next phase of development, there's a bonus: the organization builds new skills and experiences, too.

CLIENTS

While it's important to focus on your own organization's needs, serving the companies you depend on for survival is also critical. Your clients need flexibility, stability, and ultimately, proof that you'll be around for the long term—and this is especially true during the tough times. Demonstrating value clients will remember when the market picks up? That's the upside of down.

- Offer short-term flexibility. This works best if you, yourself, have the flexibility—if you are prepared and have planned. Client needs a delay on a shipment? Fine. Client needs adjustable payment terms? Got it. Client needs extra resources to make good on the plan? Of course. (You've been waiting for this moment.)

- Find creative ways to provide more value with less. Can you consolidate your deliverables? Can you collaborate differently or trade something that isn't important to you but that *is* important to the client? Can you remove an expectation—like premium packaging or an elevated ordering experience—in the short term that allows both parties to save costs?

- Help navigate difficult waters. If you are embedded in your client's business, you will have many points of contact. Because of this level of intimacy, you may see themes and trends they don't. You can help them navigate more successfully, and you can understand their challenges in ways they might not have seen or appreciated.

VENDORS

In a similar vein to your clients, your business depends on the strength of your vendor community. The upside of down here is that there's a chance to deepen those bonds while simultaneously positioning yourself as a dependable, long-term industry member.

- Maintain relationships. Renegotiating contracts or recommitting when others are shrinking speaks volumes. Vendors will remember who stayed the course, who stuck around.

- If your peers are waiting on the sidelines, watching how the market plays out, vendors in the sales, distribution, or marketing channels may get nervous. This can be a great time for you, though, to land better deals, extend payment conditions, and deepen commitments with them. And as your peers leave, you can double down on those deals that maximize advertising and revenue spending.

- Communicate early and often. As vendors look to you for reassurance, being transparent, even if it's bad news, provides certainty. This visibility can be a differentiator during uncertain times—boosting confidence in your capabilities and, ultimately, securing deeper relationships throughout the supply chain.

COMPETITORS

Capturing market share during turbulent times can be a highly impactful upside of down. As the tectonic plates of the economy shift, opportunities will arise to thin out the crowd.

- Take advantage of retreating or overextended competitors. Many times, competitors withdraw, focusing internally on processes, people, and costs instead of the client. Or maybe they are so overwhelmed by change or have shrunk their resources so much that they overwork their employees, making clients feel neglected. Either way, what happens is this: they forget to check in on the very clients who pay the bills. Stepping in with a well-timed pitch while competitors are on the back foot can fill the voids they've unintentionally created.

- Seek out alliances and acquisitions. The rules can change, often out of nowhere. Partnerships and purchases that might not fly in calmer times can often be initiated, explored, and consolidated in the rockier ones. When that happens, it can boost your long-term positioning among clients, vendors, and within the industry.

- Take a bigger piece of the pie. Just one less competitor means more market share—and hence, increased revenue once things rebound. Reductions in the competitor field may not necessarily mean short-term revenue growth, but market share capture can significantly pay off in the future. Plus, it will be harder for fragile competitors to stabilize on the other side of the storm.

Hard times can be exactly that—hard. But they don't have to be catastrophic, too, especially if you've stress-tested market correction scenarios, examined adversity in the marketplace, and outlined opportunities with your team, vendors, clients, and competitors. Beyond planning and preparation, your creativity, confidence, and courage are paramount to achieving even better results.

So don't get down—instead, look for the upside of down. It's a different test of leadership.

BE BOLD, BE BRAVE

"**W**HAT ARE YOU waiting for? Shoot!" It sure is easy to sit on the couch and shout at the athletes on television, but getting points on the scoreboard is hard. Think about it. Scoring is the result of many, many risks an athlete takes within a set system of play. The wrong move makes a player vulnerable to a turnover or a goal from the other team. They're constantly pushing against forces like the opposition's formations, tactics, and the opposing team's players, whose objective is to stop them from winning.

Like athletes, leaders are also constantly mitigating risk—a responsibility that makes up a large part of a leader's job, but whose difficulty is often underestimated by the organization. In the business world, risks may come from economic forces like supply and demand, inflation, or demographic changes. A new market entrant or a new product launch are examples of competitive risks. Other types of risk include technological risks, investment risks, financial risks, human risks, acquisition risks, and strategic positioning risks.

Like athletes, leaders also push against forces inside the organization that seek to preserve the status quo. Perhaps your organization has outdated internal processes, or a company-wide emotional attachment to a previous investment. Perhaps the company has no appetite for change, or it's saddled with an overly comfortable senior team and/or a dysfunctional board. These are the types of organizational forces that bind a company to the past, and they can be strong enough to lead to inertia and, eventually, to decay.

For you as the leader, "the buck stops here." And because you are ultimately responsible for decisions, and no decision is ever made without engendering some form of risk, you may understandably feel anxious. That's why some people at the top often prefer to stick with what has always worked.

You can try to mitigate risk. The problem is, though, that exposes you to a different kind of risk: threats in another area. For instance, if you lessen financial risk by not making an investment, you might increase strategic positioning risk, which leaves you vulnerable to losing market share. Or maybe you overreact to a human risk—say, fear of losing key employees—by over-indexing salary, bonuses, benefits. But that exposes the organization to financial risks that are hard to unwind.

Here's another pressure on the risk-taking your role as leader requires: Sometimes you must make timely decisions with suboptimal, or sometimes asymmetrical, information. It's this poor information that often causes hesitation—but the leader is the very person who needs to drive change.

BE BOLD, BE BRAVE

Author John A. Shedd said: "A ship in harbor is safe, but that is not what ships are built for."

It's the same for athletes and leaders. Athletes play to move the game forward, to take shots, to score, and hopefully, to win. Exceptional leaders have a bold vision—they imagine a way of being in the world that doesn't exist today—and a systemic bias for action—they bring that vision to life by challenging the status quo and making courageous choices. And they do all that while mitigating the risk—managing competitive threats, challenges in the workplace, and client satisfaction—while also leading disruptive change in acquisitions, new products, or developed business models.

It's a delicate balancing act. And the truth is, you might have to lean into risk-taking more than you are comfortable with. But there will come a decisive moment where the risk of doing nothing outweighs taking a calculated risk—taking a shot—and doing something.

To move the considerable forces of inertia within yourself, your team, your organization, investors, stakeholders, and the wider world, be bold with strategy and brave with action that brings it to life. Here's a start:

Be bold with strategy

- Ask for the resources you need at the beginning of your tenure. If you compromise with stakeholders and the board, even with good intention, there's only one person who suffers—you. Instead of saying, "I don't have what I want, but I think I can make it work," say this: "Here's what I need to be successful."

- Figure out what the industry needs not today, but in a few years' time. Then position the organization to deliver it right on time. Hope is not a strategy.

- Anticipate what your clients are looking for. Embed yourself inside your clients' organization (if business-to-business) or mindset (if business-to-consumer). If you know what your clients need before they do, you'll be ahead of the game.

- Determine what nobody else is doing today, something that can distinguish you as different. Maybe it's a game-changing approach that disrupts the way things have always been done, so that instead of playing the game, you are changing the rules.

Be brave with action

- Decide how quickly you move to action. That takes courage. There will be plenty of people who will tell you that it can't be done, but you need to know when to ignore them, steel yourself, and do it anyway.

- Certain elements can get in the way of speedy implementation: your existing organizational structure, your processes, colleagues, clients, location, and any legal issues, for example. Take them into consideration, but don't let the past define the future.

- Identify where you are stuck right now. Start with self-imposed constraints, then move outside of your own head to the limitations within your team and the organization. How can you unleash untapped potential and inspire people to act?

Be bold, be brave. How many leaders have expressed regret about pushing too far? How many more, though, regret not pushing hard enough—not being brave enough to make courageous choices to achieve something that matches the boldness of their vision? Now fast forward to the end of your career. What shots will you wish you had taken?

DISRUPT YOURSELF FROM THE INSIDE-OUT

THE HUMAN MIND craves stability, predictability, and order. But the belief that security can be achieved with enough money, enough power, and enough forethought is a fallacy. Life—this fragile and beautiful life—fluctuates between stability and chaos, predictability and uncertainty, and order and disorder.

You can never really hold on to feeling safe, steady, and worry-free—at least not for very long. Yet most people's mental grip fixates on grand illusions of unlimited health, financial independence, and meaningful relationships.

We think the same way about our businesses.

But life isn't all rainbows and unicorns; people change and processes ebb and flow. If you are a great leader, you'll recognize this. And you'll understand that the strengths that have taken a long time to build—like market share or relationships—can be lost in an instant. Eventually, "the world" will knock you down—even if you're used to winning.

DISRUPT YOURSELF FROM THE INSIDE-OUT

The more you acknowledge chaos, uncertainty, and disorder, the less you'll be disrupted from the outside-in. The best protection against an uncertain world is disrupting the one thing you *can* control—yourself—from the inside-out.

Professional athletes disrupt themselves from the inside-out all the time.

It's the relentless pursuit of "better" that differentiates the greatest athletes from weekend warriors. The #1 ranked golf player who modifies their swing. A top-level tennis player who deconstructs their serve after each match. A world-class football coach who changes players, formations, and systems, even as their team enjoys a winning streak.

Business leaders can disrupt themselves from the inside-out, too. Avoiding complacency and taking out insurance are two ways.

AVOIDING COMPLACENCY

Complacency is dangerous. It leaves you unaware of your surroundings and unprepared for nasty surprises. If you are unaware and unprepared, then events like a financial crisis, a business relationship blow-up, or even an unexpected health scare can have even bigger consequences.

For example, you take a long-term client relationship for granted. Initially, your communication starts to diminish. Then your attention levels dwindle. Product and service quality starts to slide. Maybe an issue arises—and when the client voices concerns you don't take them seriously or you simply rely on history to save you. This tactic works sometimes, right up until it doesn't.

Not only have you damaged a long-standing client relationship because of complacency, you've opened the door for competitors to steal in. The disruption will be worse if changes have occurred without your knowledge—your point of contact, the client's needs, or the business environment, for instance. Now you're on the back foot—unfocused and disorganized—scrambling to react from a vulnerable position.

TAKING OUT INSURANCE

We protect our life, our cars, and our houses against disaster. And by staying vigilant, preparing for uncertain times, and pushing beyond the edge, you can mitigate the impact of external disruption by safeguarding yourself professionally, too.

Stay vigilant. Keep an eye on client relationships, the industry, and the market. You'll need to continuously adapt yourself, your relationships, and your organization— internal initiatives and processes—to remain relevant.

To prepare for uncertain times, evaluate and prepare for hypothetical scenarios. Build contingencies and capacity. Being ready for whatever comes next will give you the best chance to succeed in an uncertain world.

Even when you're at the top of your game, and especially when you think you don't need it, find the edge. Then challenge yourself, your team, and your organization to push beyond it by exploring new approaches, technologies, strategy, business models, or organizational structures. What are your competitors doing that you aren't? What can you offer your clients that you haven't before?

Disrupting yourself from the inside-out takes time, energy, and resources. But avoiding complacency and taking out insurance is worth the effort, if only for the peace of mind that you've created a buffer between you and the worst the world may throw at you; that you are focused, prepared, and ready for anything. Bring it on!

A LEADER IS EVERYTHING THEY ARE NOT

THERE'S A WELL-KNOWN meditation exercise that asks people to hold, and eventually eat, a single raisin, while mindfully engaging each sense. But there's another part of this meditation that involves appreciating the conditions— seen and unseen—that brought the raisin into being. It might look something like this:

- Visualize the grape that was dried to create the raisin.

- Imagine the grape vine that produced the grape.

- Consider the soil that sustained the vine.

- Reflect on how weather elements contributed to the vine's chances of survival. The water and sun that fed it; the wind that bent the vine into a shape that protects its bounty; how it was spared from frost damage.

- Think about the predator that sniffed the bunch of grapes and moved on to the next bunch, leaving the grape intact.

- Envision the farmer who watered the vine during a drought, and who pruned branches and twigs so the energy vital to its development remained intact and concentrated.

- And what about all the other people that encountered the grape or raisin as it made its way to the present moment? The laborer who picked the grape, for example. The factory worker who washed and dehydrated the grape to make the raisin. The person who packed the raisin into a box, and another who loaded the boxes onto the truck, whose driver traveled to a local market or across the country. The store worker or market stall owner who presented the raisins for you to purchase.

The raisin physically exists as a raisin, but you can also see the raisin as everything it is *physically* not. In other words, the raisin is made up of those conditions—seen and unseen—that brought it into the world and into your hand. And when you consider that, a single raisin takes on real significance. It becomes a thing of wonder, a window into the beauty and fragility of our interconnected lives.

And if you're a leader, you might even appreciate the parallels between the raisin's unique journey and your own.

A leader is everything they are not. Meaning, just like the raisin, you are also made up of the conditions—seen and unseen, hardy or fertile—that affected your personal development. A meditation about what brought you into being might look something like this:

- Visualize the ancestors that came before you.

- Imagine the parents who created you.

- Reflect on how your foundational needs were met as a child. Water and food. Shelter. Friends and family.

- Think about dangerous people who thought about harming you but moved on to something else, leaving you intact.

- Envision the people who supported you during tough times, and believed in you so much that it helped you stay confident, energized, and whole. Now envision the experiences that "pruned" you, enabling you to draw in vital energy to thrive.

- And how about all the other people you've encountered? A favorite teacher or sports coach who saw your untapped potential. Your first job out of college where a judgmental and temperamental boss taught you how *not* to lead. An overseas posting that forced you to ask for help, as you learned a new culture and language. A challenging project that yielded underwhelming yet highly visible results.

A personal benefit of this meditation exercise may be a greater appreciation for your distinctive journey and the people who helped you thrive. What might follow is a renewed lust for life because your story isn't over yet—what uplifting news!

Giving thanks for your personal journey can help you appreciate others' journeys, too. This could mean working in an intentional, empathetic way: listening to team members' distinctive experiences; creating an environment where sharing builds bonds, learning from each other; designing cohesive and inclusive approaches to challenges.

Your organization can also benefit, particularly if you build out leadership development programs that push people outside of their function, geography, culture, and expertise. It will help everyone gain insights they might not otherwise physically observe and challenge them to learn outside of a routine or familiar approach.

When we reflect on what *we are not*, it can lead to a deeper recognition and a renewed appreciation for *what we are*. How we integrate these learnings into what *we will be*, well, that's the ongoing work of leadership, the ongoing work of life—this sweet and delicious life.

CONSCIOUS LEADERSHIP

DEVELOPMENTS IN SCIENCE and technology have made an easier life possible. But technological innovation can have unintended, distasteful consequences as well.

According to researchers, we're bombarded by over thirty-four gigabytes of content and 100,000 words of information every day. That's enough to overload a laptop in a week! And although the brain is a sophisticated processing machine, it struggles to consistently perform at this level. Digesting, processing, synthesizing—simplifying the modern world's complexity to make good decisions—becomes harder. It's exhausting and unsustainable work, especially for leaders who want to shape the future.

The good news is that the conditions are ripe for an evolution in leadership—it's called conscious leadership. If you are a conscious leader, you experience life without the distorting lens of judgment, seeing the world as it really is. You move away from the self-oriented (egoic) nature of your mind, body, and emotions toward a higher state of awareness that allows you to focus on serving others and the larger world.

Conscious leadership is not a spiritual quest. You've got a business to run, after all. But if you follow its principles, here's what's in for you:

- Because you've increased your awareness, you'll filter information—those thirty-four gigabytes of content and 100,000 words of information every day—better. You'll have increased clarity to make higher quality and more informed decisions.

- Because you've elevated yourself from the day-to-day noise at the ground level, you'll be less distracted by it. You'll see the bigger patterns at play, and it will be easier for you to simplify complexity.

- Because a conscious leadership approach is not about you—but rather, it's other-centric—you'll evolve into someone who's able to shape a future that celebrates balance, joy, and aliveness… for everyone.

And what that means for your business is this: employees who are more grounded, happier, and more engaged in their work.

If you want to grow your conscious leadership practice, create the conditions: Do the deeper work to develop your self-awareness, practice an intentional way of being, and focus on vertical development.

DEVELOP YOUR SELF-AWARENESS

Psychometric assessment tools indicate how you show up in, or see, the world. You can complement that data with feedback about the external behaviors that others observe. In other words, how the world sees you.

A guide—such as a trained coach, a therapist, or a psychologist—can help you see how your external behaviors connect to the inner world you've constructed from your personal preferences and orientation (nature), your early experiences (nurture), and the stories you tell yourself (narrative).

Conscious leaders make deeper self-awareness a priority. And for this potentially transformational work, there are no specific "tools." You simply must get out of your own way and get out of your own head. Why? So that you can see yourself from the outside-in, which allows you to manage your behaviors and channel your emotional energy where it is most needed.

PRACTICE AN INTENTIONAL WAY OF BEING

There's no guaranteed playbook for running a business, especially in challenging times. Of course, there are common principles that can guide you, but nothing can fully prepare you for something you've never done before, especially when the stakes are high. Even if you have a Ph.D. specializing in "leading through crisis," for instance, the actual (not theoretical) experience of performing that hard work in the moment is unique—because every business is unique, every leader is unique, every team is unique, and every crisis is unique.

Most leaders spend their time in "doing" mode, rarely in reflection or "being" mode. Intentional contemplation is integral to conscious leadership because it's a way to gain wisdom and discover universal truths. Taking time to understand the unique set of circumstances you are facing, while also drawing from relevant past experiences, can help you confidently set the best path forward.

A "doing more and doing faster" attitude makes an already fast-paced world feel extra intense. Imagine your work calendar, for example. It's probably full of back-to-back meetings about different issues with various levels of complexity, importance, and expectation, right? Each one of those meetings requires intricate back-and-forths, the stuff of relationships—relationships that contain subtleties of human connection, motivation, and other emotional drivers—that you then process through your own perspective with all your own baggage. No wonder you often feel stressed and exhausted!

Reflection puts a not-doing break in your day. It's slowing down to think about the things that have been done. Instead of stepping into a state of "doing," you're stepping back to absorb the bigger picture. You're seeing how the larger systems operate and how you play a part in them, so that when it's time to act, your consciousness—your awareness—is elevated, and you can take a more strategic pathway.

FOCUS ON VERTICAL DEVELOPMENT

In leadership terms, horizontal development is growth that comes from your interaction with the outer world. It's about *what* you know, what you've acquired—skills, knowledge, facts, and capabilities. Traditional leadership theory and training is rooted in this idea.

Vertical development focuses on your inner world: personal growth drawn from learning, experiences, and insights. It involves understanding how your own perspectives, preferences, and experiences contribute to, and also limit, your worldview. It's *how* you know—and this can lead to alternative worldviews, advanced frameworks, and evolved mindsets.

Ultimately, a vertically developed leader is more mature, more wise, and more evolved.

A way to explain the difference is this: Horizontal development is like filling up a vessel with more water (i.e., skills, knowledge, facts, and capabilities) whereas vertical development is like expanding the size of the vessel (i.e., increased worldviews, developed frameworks, evolved mindsets).

A conscious leader has both. So that in any given situation, they are able to operate with increased awareness, draw from multiple perspectives, and consider situations through advanced frameworks in a way that makes them less reactive and more responsive.

Buddhist monk and teacher Thich Nhat Hanh said: "We have the tendency to think in terms of doing and not in terms of being. We think that when we are not doing anything, we are wasting our time. That is not true. Our time is first of all for us to be. To be what? To be alive, to be peace, to be joy, to be loving. And that is what the world needs the most."

You can react to this frantic world by moving faster, consuming more, and doing extra.

But perhaps what we need more than anything else is to stop doing and start being. Maybe that's what this modern world is saying it needs the most.

WHAT GREAT
LEADERS DO

WE'RE USED TO thinking about great leaders as grandiose, dominant, decisive, and self-oriented; as individuals unceasingly driven by a singular, unforgiving, all-consuming vision. These days, the world requires a different kind of leader. And the great ones lead in some of the following ways.

GREAT LEADERS...
STAY HUMBLE WHILE
ACCOMPLISHING
GREAT THINGS

"Egoless confidence," in a business context, means that you as the leader believe in yourself, *and* you believe in others.

Your confidence is not based only on yourself. It's not just "I believe in me," it's "I believe in us."

If you have egoless confidence, you respond to what the situation calls for rather than what you want, what you are competent at, or what your training and experience prescribe. You put your own desires to one side. You focus on others.

If you are other-focused, your mindset is, "When things go well it is down to my team; when things go badly it is down to me." You're effectively shielding your team against unnecessary, distracting criticism, and having faith that they will figure out the next steps behind closed doors—and most importantly, do better next time. And you're also promoting team autonomy while creating the conditions for greater accountability. All highly desirable outcomes.

GREAT LEADERS... ELEVATE THEMSELVES THROUGH SELF-AWARENESS

Knowing your strengths and when/how to compensate for your weaknesses are hallmarks of greatness. That means you know when to step in and lead and when to step back and follow; or when to trust the process and watch a plan that you set in motion come to life.

You cannot live up to your fullest potential until you have looked inwardly. It can be hard work—extremely hard. But it pays off in remarkable ways. When you are vulnerable, especially with your own weaknesses, it teaches others to do the same. There's a domino effect: great leader, great team, great organization.

GREAT LEADERS... BALANCE REASON AND PASSION

A reliance on cold reason alone can steer you toward heartlessness. A cold, overly rational and callous analysis of the data can lead to decision-making that underestimates impacts on people inside the organization. It treats people as numbers—and nothing else.

Ultimately, relying on reason alone creates a toxic, unfriendly, and inhuman culture that forgets that the basis of an organization (and its success) is people. And people are what move the organization forward.

And what about passion? It can be the fuel for inspiration—or the flame that burns down everyone and everything around it. Think of leaders who become agitated in a critical client situation; who don't keep their emotions in check when making decisions or managing people; or who regularly use emotion to manipulate circumstances.

Ultimately, too much passion can desensitize a team to truly urgent situations, gutting the potential power of any future well-timed emotional intervention. Worse, over time, a leader's emotionally charged behavior may create a serious lack of clarity and consistency—meaning, that the person who is supposed to be in charge isn't taken seriously.

Kahlil Gibran said, "Your reason and your passion are the rudder and the sails of your seafaring soul." Using their head and their heart, great leaders balance the clarity and power of reason with the emotive energy of passion to masterfully steer their organization to sunnier shores.

GREAT LEADERS... UNLOCK LEADERSHIP IN OTHERS

You have probably worked for a leader who showed you how *not* to lead. And in contrast, if you are lucky, you also have worked for a leader—hopefully, leaders—who saw potential in you that you didn't see yourself.

Great leaders place confidence in their team members and give them room to make mistakes. In the aftermath of failure, a great leader will put an arm around a colleague's shoulder, and then take it a step further: help them learn a lesson. It's this giving out of tough-but-fair feedback that speaks volumes. "I believe in you enough to care" might just encourage them to come back stronger next time.

GREAT LEADERS... FORGIVE, BUT THEY DON'T FORGET

Most people don't come to work to mess up, or to make things worse. Usually, if something goes wrong there is a lack of communication, understanding, or capability. Great leaders look beyond the headline. They offer the benefit of the doubt and make time to find out what really happened.

Great leaders forgive the person but won't forget the mistake. By sharing constructive feedback, you can demonstrate that for the most part, mistakes are rarely fatal. Such compassion and generosity can turn simple, transactional interactions into something more transformative. In high-risk situations you may not have the luxury of a second chance, but you can still help your team find learnings in loss.

GREAT LEADERS... LEAD WITH LOVE

Great leaders love:

- Who they are and what they do.

- Their team, their organization, and their clients.

- Finding the best in others and finding the teachings in failure.

- Achieving success and celebrating with their teams.

- Leading with love.

The great leaders of the modern world demonstrate humility and self-awareness. Balancing reason and passion, unlocking leadership in others, showing forgiveness, and leading with love—all these are not just how great leaders lead, but ultimately who they are. Who wouldn't want to work with a leader who shows up like this?

And wouldn't you want to be that kind of leader? Today that might be an aspiration but what's stopping you? Nothing. Let's Go!

LET'S GO!

NOTHING EVER LASTS forever, as the song goes.

Countries and their governments. Cities and towns. Buildings and parks. Your clients and your industry. Your organization and your colleagues. Your friends and family. Your successes and failures. Your security and well-being. Your happiness and unhappiness.

You.

Life is impermanent, we know this. Yet there is something in the human mind that yearns for permanence. That responds to certainty. That craves structure, systems, processes, and predictable outcomes. That pretends the second law of thermodynamics, which is all about entropy—uncertainty, disorder, decay—doesn't exist.

But it does.

And what it means is that within any system, nothing remains the same. That change is constant. That, without external energy invested into a system, everything will gradually decline. And eventually die or disappear.

Countries and their governments. Cities and towns. Buildings and parks. Your clients and your industry. Your organization and your colleagues. Your friends and family. Your successes and failures. Your security and well-being. Your happiness and unhappiness.

Our lives are like castles made from sand. It takes so much more energy to create and maintain them than to erode and destroy them.

Painting a picture, building a business, legislating for a municipality, writing a book, raising a child—before you even start, you know things may go badly wrong—or you may fail completely. And even if it does go right, the good stuff likely won't last for long.

So why reach forward into an uncertain, disordered, decaying—and impermanent—future to make something of significance if you're working against natural physical laws?

Because that's the essence of being alive, this ultimate act of defiance against an often intransigent and insensible universe. And your willingness to leave your mark on an uncertain, disordered, decaying—impermanent— future? Well, perhaps that's the greatest act of humanity.

So let's go, leaders.

Be a Role Model. Develop your self-awareness and use it to inspire others.

Be a Community Builder. Create a sense of belonging. Bring together like-minded people, galvanize a group around a specific goal, and develop cohesiveness, connection, and collaboration. Build your crew.

Be a Sense Maker. Use your knowledge, insight, and experience to understand and explain the world. Rely on your sense of meaning to codify information, organize thoughts, and guide behaviors.

Be a Future Shaper. Use your sense of purpose to ignite others around a common goal. Take us out of the mundane. Inspire us to be the best versions of ourselves. Provide us with the tools to change and grow. Encourage us to imagine and build a better world.

Give us a reason to live.

You can do what great leaders do. So let's go, leaders. Let's go!

PULLING TOGETHER THE FOUR DIMENSIONS OF LEADERSHIP

THANKS FOR JOINING me on this leadership journey. I hope you are inspired, fired up, and ready to go. To bring this book full circle, let's do one final high-level review of the four timeless dimensions of leadership—also known as the four leadership roles—that are so deeply linked to the universal human needs for a sense of self, belonging, meaning, and purpose.

ROLE MODEL

Through <u>consistency</u> and <u>integrity</u>, a leader models behavior that reflects the values and principles of the people they represent. They build trust through their actions, and they embody the essential character of the group or organization.

Why is the Role Model important? We look to leaders to manifest our values and principles. We need them to be the best version of themselves. When that happens, it inspires us to be our best selves. This leadership role helps satisfy a universal human need—a sense of self.

COMMUNITY BUILDER

The leader combines a <u>focus on others</u>, along with advanced <u>communication</u> skills to create cohesiveness and connectivity within the group. Leaders will take time to reflect on individual drivers—what makes someone tick? what gets them excited?—as well as collective dynamics to inspire and motivate team members to live up to their fullest potential.

Why is the Community Builder important? Because great leaders give us a forum for connection, an opportunity to feel part of something bigger than ourselves. And that nourishes one of our most basic human needs—a sense of belonging.

SENSE MAKER

The world can be an unpredictable place. But a leader makes sense of the world for themselves and their followers through <u>intelligence</u> and a <u>learning orientation</u>. Especially in times of great uncertainty, this capability is rare and precious. Leaders help us organize thoughts, anticipate change, challenge conventions, identify invisible forces, and codify the world.

Why is the Sense Maker important? When the world throws shocks and thunderbolts our way, leaders help us understand what's happening. Leaders provide a framework that makes tumultuous events and invisible forces clear, comprehensible, and manageable. Understanding *why* nurtures a universal human need—a sense of meaning.

FUTURE SHAPER

The leader sees and shapes the future through their <u>vision</u> and <u>bias for action</u>. Their strategic orientation galvanizes the group and drives transformation. They give us something to aspire to: a future where we can be part of something bigger than ourselves. And that future, once realized, becomes the leader's legacy.

Why is the Future Shaper important? At the heart of all great movements and all great institutions is a group of people who have imagined a better world, a group in which each person has contributed to something they could not have accomplished alone. The leader has activated and satisfied another universal human need—a sense of purpose.

LET'S GO!

In the end, this is all about you and what you are capable of doing. And make no mistake: You are capable. What you've read in this book? You can do it.

You can develop the integrity and consistency to become a role model for others.

You can learn to focus on those around you and hone your communication skills to build community.

You can lean into learning and sharpen your cognitive, social, and emotional intelligence to make sense of the world for others.

You can exercise and strengthen your bias for action. You can develop a compelling vision worthy of fighting for.

You can do what great leaders do. You can shape the future.

So let's go, leaders. Let's go!

ACKNOWLEDGMENTS

JEAN RAMSDEN co-authored this book. Over the last 25 years, we've collaborated on marriage, parenthood, creative projects, business, and more—and I wouldn't do any of it with anyone else.

My grandmother, Lilley Ramsden, was a force of nature who proved, through compassion and a will to make things better, that leadership has no defining age, guise, or gender.

Adam and JoJo have always loved and supported me unconditionally. I'm lucky to be their brother.

Life is better with people who make you laugh, cheer you on, and keep you humble—like Colin Maduzia, The La's (Justin and Dennis), BTV (Ads, Ed, Chris, and Andy), Jon Hourihan, and CJ.

Andrew Robshaw was a life-changing mentor. George Owen, Chris Jenks, and Stuart Goodridge took a chance on me. Jonathan Kirschner's continued partnership is a gift.

Lancaster University Management School professor Stephen Kempster helped me navigate the academic world of leadership. Francesca White has stuck with me from the beginning.

It's rare to be given silent space to harness your own power. Namaste, Amy Schneider.

I would like to acknowledge the following coaches who have provided insight, guidance, and camaraderie: Glenn Newsom, Peter Hazelrigg, Stephanie Lischke, Andre Keil, Chuck Ainsworth, Kara Penfeld, Jennifer Hall, Sara King, Johan Naudé, Ren Wiebe, Manuelle Charbonneau, Bernadette Cabrera, Bob Kinnison, David Yudis, Lynn Ellen Queen, and Michelle Braden.

Haydn Hasty, who unlocked the world beyond the physical for me, continues to make me a better coach.

Thank you to my clients, who have allowed me to be part of their journeys. I am especially grateful to the unnamed CEO who opened his heart and cried on my shoulder in an Alpine hotel a quarter of a century ago—and revealed my future path without knowing it.

Special thanks to Myles Hunt, Sally Tickner, Nick Fletcher, Chris Parker, Lucy Scott, and Elena Jones at Harriman House.

Paul Damiano, Ph.D., who served as technical advisor, is an inspiration and a friend. The incomparable Katherine Catmull put tremendous care into the book's development.

This book is a gift to Harmonie, Keegan, Bodie, and Sawyer, who gave Jean and I the freedom to write. As you continue to shape your own futures, we hope these ideas will guide you along the way.

INDEX

ABOUT THE AUTHOR

J AMIE RAMSDEN IS a
former CEO with 25 years of
international business experience.
As an elite coach, he works with
Fortune 500 C-suite clients,
business owners, and entrepreneurs
across the globe to drive consistent,
sustainable results through strategy,
people development, and scalable infrastructure. His
inspirational approach to leadership is shaped by extensive
practical business knowledge, deep insights into human
motivations, and his proprietary leadership framework.

Using ideas drawn from his research, his work as a CEO,
and his elite-level coaching, Jamie has written extensively
about leadership and executive coaching. He trained at

the Center for Creative Leadership and is certified by the International Coach Federation. Jamie holds an MBA with a specialization in leadership and change management from Lancaster University (UK).

Jamie challenges clients to tap into their own business and life experiences to unlock profound insights. Those insights translate into action that builds lasting professional and personal success. Guided by his framework, clients become role models, community builders, and sense makers, not only for themselves but for their teams and organizations. Most importantly, he motivates executives to shape the future—the real work of leadership.